Contents Guide

~ Welcome & What You'll Learn

Section 4: Empowering Command Prowess

Section 5: Crafting Custom Commands

Section 6: Advanced Command-Line Techniques

~ Conclusion

Welcome & What You'll Learn

The Gateway to Linux Mastery

Welcome, intrepid explorer, to the exhilarating world of the Linux command line! If you're ready to unlock the true power of your Linux system, shed the limitations of graphical interfaces, and transform your computing experience, then you've arrived at the perfect place.

This book is your comprehensive guide, a meticulously crafted map designed to lead you from curious adventurer to seasoned Linux command-line master. Whether you're a newcomer to the world of Linux or a seasoned user seeking to deepen your knowledge, this book will empower you with the skills, secrets, and techniques to elevate your command-line proficiency.

Why the Command Line?

In a world dominated by flashy buttons and intuitive menus, you might be wondering, "Why bother with the command line at all?" Let's illuminate the compelling reasons:

- **Unmatched Power:** The command line grants you unparalleled control over your Linux system. Tasks that might require a labyrinth of clicks and menus within a graphical environment can often be executed with a single, well-crafted command.
- **Efficiency and Speed:** Once you master the language of the command line, you'll discover breathtaking speed and efficiency. Your fingers will dance across the keyboard, issuing commands that streamline workflows and accomplish tasks in mere moments.
- **Automation:** The command line is the key to automation. Imagine scripts that tirelessly perform complex, repetitive tasks on your behalf, freeing your time and energy for greater pursuits.
- **Remote Access:** Need to manage a server halfway across the globe? The command line is your indispensable tool. Connect remotely, diagnose issues, and implement solutions as if you were physically present.
- **Customization:** Linux is renowned for its incredible flexibility. The command line epitomizes this, inviting you to tailor your system precisely to your needs and preferences.

The Journey Ahead

Buckle up, because we're about to embark on an extraordinary adventure! This book systematically breaks down the intricate realm of the Linux command line into clear, digestible segments. Here's a glimpse of what you'll learn:

- **Navigating the Terrain:** You'll become intimately familiar with the Linux filesystem, traversing directories with effortless grace and uncovering hidden files with ease.
- **Manipulating Files and Directories:** You'll master the art of creating, moving, deleting, and copying files and directories – the core building blocks of file management.
- **Text Manipulation Mastery:** Edit text files directly from the command line, search for patterns, and reshape data streams into the exact output you desire.
- **Unlocking Command Potential:** You'll delve into the vast library of commands at your disposal, learning how to seek help, combine commands for maximum impact, and unleash the power of wildcards.
- **Customization and Automation:** Discover how to bend the command line to your will, creating aliases, crafting custom commands, and scripting repetitive tasks to streamline your workflow.
- **Advanced Techniques:** You'll ascend to new heights of command-line mastery, exploring system monitoring, networking tools, performance optimization, and other powerful techniques to maximize your Linux proficiency.

The Learning Approach

This book isn't merely a theoretical treatise. It's a hands-on, experiential journey. Throughout the chapters, you'll be guided through a wealth of practical examples and exercises designed to reinforce your understanding and solidify your skills. We firmly believe that the best way to learn the command line is by *doing*, not just reading.

Let's Begin!

Are you ready to leave the realm of mere user and become a Linux power user? Excellent! Turn the page, open your terminal, and let the adventure commence!

Additional Resources

- **The Linux Documentation Project:** A fantastic resource for deepening your Linux knowledge: https://tldp.org/
- **Linux man pages:** Access these built-in help pages directly in your terminal with commands like man ls

Section 1:
Introduction to the Command Line

Embarking on Your Linux Journey: Initiating the Terminal Experience

Welcome to the gateway of true Linux power – the terminal. This window into the heart of your operating system might seem daunting at first, with its blinking cursor and lack of colorful icons. However, fear not! In this chapter, we'll begin demystifying the terminal, transforming it from an unknown wilderness into a landscape of limitless possibilities.

What is the Terminal?

Let's break down the basics:

- **The Command-Line Interface (CLI):** The terminal is your direct connection to the command-line interface. This text-based interface allows you to control your Linux system by issuing typed commands rather than clicking on graphical elements.
- **The Shell:** Within the terminal operates a program called the shell. It interprets the commands you type, communicates with the deeper layers of the operating system, and presents you with the results. Popular Linux shells include Bash, Zsh, and Fish.
- **GUI vs. CLI:** Think of your Linux system as having two faces. One is the Graphical User Interface (GUI), the world of windows, menus, and clickable icons you're likely familiar with. The terminal offers an alternative way to interact with the same system, favoring precision and power over visual simplicity.

Finding Your Terminal

The way you access your terminal will depend slightly on your specific Linux distribution. Here's how to find it in some common environments:

- **GNOME Desktop:** Look for an application usually named "Terminal" or "Konsole" (if you're using KDE Plasma) within your application menu.

- **Other Desktop Environments:** Most Linux desktops provide a similar way to access the terminal through their applications list.
- **Keyboard Shortcut:** A reliable shortcut common to many systems is "Ctrl + Alt + T".

Once you've launched the terminal, you'll be greeted with a simple window featuring some text (likely your username and computer name) followed by a blinking cursor. This is where the adventure begins!

Your First Commands

Let's get comfortable with a few basic commands to navigate this new world:

- **pwd (Print Working Directory):** This command reveals where you are in the Linux file system. Think of it as the GPS coordinates of your current location. For example, typing pwd might output /home/yourusername.
- **ls (List Contents):** Use this command to see the files and directories (folders) within your current location.
- **cd <directory_name> (Change Directory):** This is your key to moving around the file system. For example, cd Documents would move you into the "Documents" directory within your home folder.

Important Notes:

- **Linux is case-sensitive:** documents is not the same as Documents. Pay attention to capitalization!
- **The Power of Tab:** The Tab key is your friend! Start typing a command or filename, hit Tab, and the terminal will often autocomplete it for you, saving time and preventing typos.

Beyond the Basics

We've only scratched the surface! Here's a sneak peek of what you'll learn in upcoming chapters:

- **File System Navigation:** Become an expert in traversing directories, understanding paths, and using shortcuts like .. (to go one level up) and ~ (to represent your home directory).
- **Creating and Deleting:** Learn to create new files and directories, and how to remove them when necessary.

- **Exploring Permissions:** Uncover the system that controls who can read, write, and execute files, ensuring your system stays safe.

The Adventure Continues

Think of this chapter as base camp. We've covered the essentials of finding your terminal and issuing your first basic commands. As we progress through the book, you'll gain the skills to conquer this thrilling new terrain. Be patient, experiment, don't be afraid to break things (within a safe environment), and most importantly, have fun!

Additional Resources

- **Linux Journey:** A fantastic beginner-friendly website: https://linuxjourney.com/
- **ExplainShell:** Breaks down complex commands into easy-to-understand parts: https://explainshell.com/

Commanding Your Linux Arsenal: Essential Basics Unveiled

In the previous chapter, we opened the door to the terminal. Now, it's time to survey the array of commands at your disposal and learn how to wield them effectively. Think of this chapter as your introductory training session in a vast armory – soon, you'll be selecting the perfect tool for any task with the confidence of a seasoned warrior.

Understanding Command Structure

Let's break down the anatomy of a typical Linux command:

command_name options arguments

- **command_name:** The core instruction you're giving the system (e.g., ls, cd, pwd).
- **options:** Modifiable flags that change the command's behavior (often preceded by a single or double dash, like -l or --help).
- **arguments:** Additional inputs, such as filenames or directories, the command acts upon.

Note: Not all commands utilize all three components! Some are simple, standalone actions.

Essential Commands for Your Arsenal

Let's focus on a core set of commands you'll reach for time and time again:

1. **man (Manual Pages):** The ultimate reference guide built into your system. Type man <command_name> (e.g., man ls) to get detailed instructions and explanations on any command.
2. **echo:** A versatile tool that prints text to the terminal. Use it for testing, displaying variables, or as part of more complex scripts. For example, echo "Hello, Linux world!"
3. **clear:** Need a clean slate? This command wipes your terminal window clean.
4. **history:** Displays a list of your previously used commands. This is invaluable for recalling commands and finding patterns in your usage.

5. **mkdir (Make Directory):** Your tool for creating new directories (folders). Example: `mkdir Documents`
6. **rmdir (Remove Directory):** The counterpart to `mkdir`, this command deletes empty directories. (For directories with files inside, you'll need the more powerful `rm`)
7. **touch:** Creates an empty file or updates the timestamp of an existing file. Try `touch newfile.txt`
8. **cat (Concatenate):** A multi-purpose command frequently used to display the contents of files. For instance, `cat shoppinglist.txt`
9. **cp (Copy):** Creates copies of files. Example: `cp report.txt report_backup.txt`
10. **mv (Move):** Moves or renames files and directories. Use it like `mv oldfile.txt newfile.txt` or `mv Documents/ report.txt`

Harnessing the Power of Options

Many of these commands become truly potent when combined with options. Remember, you can always use the man command to explore your options! Let's look at a common example, the `ls` command:

- `ls` – Lists files and directories in the most basic format.
- `ls -l` – Provides a long format listing with details like file size, permissions, and modification dates.
- `ls -a` – Reveals hidden files (those starting with a .)
- `ls -R` - Performs a recursive listing, showing the contents of subdirectories too.

Putting It into Practice

Let's solidify this with a few tasks:

1. **Task:** Display a detailed listing of all files, including hidden ones, in your home directory.
   - **Solution:** `ls -la ~`
2. **Task:** Create a new directory called "Projects" and create a text file named "ideas.txt" inside it.
   - **Solution:**
     - `mkdir Projects`
     - `cd Projects`

- ■ `touch ideas.txt`
3. **Task:** View the last 20 commands you've used.
    - ○ **Solution:** `history | tail -n 20` (We'll cover the `tail` command and the | symbol in later chapters!)

Words of Caution

The command line is powerful, so proceed thoughtfully, especially when it comes to deleting files or modifying system settings. Double-check your commands before hitting Enter!

Next Steps

This chapter gave you a vital foundation. In upcoming chapters, we'll delve into navigating your Linux system's file structure, mastering file manipulation, and unlocking even more powerful commands that will transform the way you interact with your computer.

Additional Resources

- **LinuxCommand.org:** A beginner-friendly site: https://linuxcommand.org/

Deciphering the Linux Landscape, Part 1: Navigating the File System Terrain

In this chapter, "Deciphering the Linux Landscape, Part 1: Navigating the File System Terrain," we'll illuminate the organized structure upon which everything on your system is built.

The Hierarchical File System

Imagine your Linux system as a giant, upside-down tree:

- **The Root (/):** The base of this tree, the starting point of your entire file system. Every single file and directory stems from this root.
- **Directories:** The branches of this tree. Directories are like folders, designed to contain files or other directories, creating a structured organization.
- **Files:** The leaves of the tree. They hold data – text documents, images, programs, and everything else on your system.

Key Directories

Within this tree, some key directories hold special purposes:

- /home: Houses the home directories of regular users. Your personal files are likely stored within a directory under /home.
- /bin and /usr/bin: Contain essential command binaries (executable programs).
- /etc: Stores system-wide configuration files.
- /dev: Holds device files, which represent hardware components in your system.
- /tmp: A space for temporary files, often cleared automatically on reboot.

Absolute vs. Relative Paths

How do you pinpoint a specific file's location in this structure? That's where paths come in

- **Absolute Paths:** These paths begin with the root (/) and specify the complete route from the top of the file system to the desired file or

directory. For example:
`/home/yourusername/Documents/report.txt`

- **Relative Paths:** These describe locations relative to your current working directory. For instance, if you're in `/home/yourusername`, you could refer to `Documents/report.txt`

Navigation Commands – Your Essential Toolkit

You already know some core commands from the previous chapter. Let's recap and add a few more:

- **pwd (Print Working Directory):** Reveals your current location.
- **ls (List):** Lists the contents of a directory.
- **cd (Change Directory):** Your key for traveling through the system. Example: `cd /home/yourusername/Downloads`
- **.. (Parent Directory):** A special shortcut to move one level *up* the tree.
- **~ (Home Directory):** A convenient shortcut representing your own home directory.

Putting It into Practice

Let's imagine you have a photo named 'vacation.jpg' located in your 'Pictures' directory, which resides within your home directory. Here's how the concepts translate:

- **Absolute Path:** `/home/yourusername/Pictures/vacation.jpg`
- **Navigating there (from anywhere):** `cd /home/yourusername/Pictures`
- **Listing files once you arrive:** `ls`
- **Relative Path (from your home directory):** `Pictures/vacation.jpg`

Tips and Tricks

- **Tab Completion:** Your best friend! Start typing a directory or file name, then hit the Tab key to have the terminal try and complete it for you. This saves time and reduces potential errors.
- **Clarity with Long Paths:** A command like `ls /home/yourusername/Documents/Projects/ImportantFiles`

can become cumbersome. Break it down with multiple cd commands for smoother navigation.

The Adventure Continues

This chapter gave you the map and compass for navigating the Linux file system. In the next chapter, we'll go deeper, exploring techniques to see hidden files, create file structures, and understand the crucial concept of permissions.

Additional Resources

- **Explainshell.com:** Breaks down complex commands with clear examples: https://explainshell.com/
- **Filenames and Paths in Linux:** A guide from the Linux Documentation Project: https://tldp.org/LDP/intro-linux/html/sect_03_01.html

Remember, practice makes perfect! Open a terminal and start exploring your own Linux system. The more you navigate, the more natural it will become.

Deciphering the Linux Landscape, Part 2: Traversing Deeper into File System Structures

In this chapter, we'll uncover hidden realms within your file system, build new pathways, and understand the crucial concept that safeguards your Linux environment—permissions.

Unmasking the Hidden

Linux employs a clever design—some files and directories remain hidden by default to prevent accidental changes to critical system components. Let's unveil them:

- **Hidden Files and Directories:** Any file or directory starting with a dot (`.`) is hidden under normal circumstances. For instance, your home directory likely contains `.config` (for storing configuration files) and `.bashrc` (stores settings for your shell).
- **The Power of `ls -a`:** Modify the `ls` command with the `-a` option (stands for 'all') to display all files and directories, including those stealthy hidden ones.

Building Your Structure with `mkdir`

It's time to expand your Linux landscape:

- **`mkdir` (Make Directory):** Your fundamental tool for creating new directories (folders). For example, `mkdir Photos` would create a 'Photos' directory in your current location.
- **Nested Creation:** Need a more elaborate structure? No problem! A command like `mkdir -p Projects/2024/ClientA` creates all the necessary parent directories in one swift action.

The Importance of Permissions

The Linux file system isn't a free-for-all. Permissions form a security system, controlling who can do what to your files and directories. Let's break it down:

- **User, Group, and Others:** Linux associates each file with an owner (user), a group, and gives permissions for everyone else ('others').

- **Read, Write, and Execute (rwx):** The three fundamental permissions:
  - *Read (r)*: Grants the ability to view a file's contents.
  - *Write (w)*: Allows modification or deletion of a file or files within a directory.
  - *Execute (x)*: For files, it means the ability to run them as programs. For directories, it's needed to enter the directory or access files within it.

Note: Understanding how to view and change permissions is a bit more advanced, so we'll cover those techniques in a later chapter dedicated to file manipulation!

Navigating Upwards with ..

Remember this special shortcut:

- **.. (Parent Directory):** Using `cd ..` within your terminal will always take you one level up the directory tree, making navigation a breeze.

Practice Time

Let's imagine you want to organize your work:

1. **Task:** Create a directory structure within your home directory for Projects, with the year as a subdirectory, and a further subdirectory for a hypothetical 'SuperProject'.
   Solution:
   - `cd ~` (Ensure you start in your home directory)
   - `mkdir -p Projects/2024/SuperProject`
2. **Task:** You've downloaded a few interesting articles from the web into your 'Downloads' directory. They're cluttering up the space, so you want to create a 'Readings' directory inside 'Documents' and move them there.
   Solution:
   - `cd ~/Documents`
   - `mkdir Readings`
   - `cd ../Downloads` (Jump to Downloads)
   - `mv *.pdf Readings/` (This assumes your articles are PDF files)

Pro Tip: If you're unsure of your current location, the pwd command is your lifeline!

Beyond the Basics

We've only just begun exploring the depths of the Linux file system. In upcoming chapters, we'll discuss:

- Mastering file and directory manipulation with precision.
- Understanding the powerful concepts of links (both hard and soft).
- Demystifying advanced navigation techniques for seamless traversal.

Additional Resources

- **Linux File Permissions:** A detailed breakdown:
  https://linuxize.com/post/linux-file-permissions/
- **The Linux Filesystem Hierarchy Structure:**
  https://www.tldp.org/LDP/Linux-Filesystem-Hierarchy/html/

Charting Your Course Through Linux, Part 1: Mastering Navigation Techniques

Let's dive into the next stage of your journey with "Charting Your Course Through Linux, Part 1: Mastering Navigation Techniques." Think of this chapter like upgrading your simple map to a powerful GPS, giving you pinpoint accuracy and flexibility as you traverse your Linux system.

Key Navigation Commands (Recap)

Before we go deeper, let's refresh our memory on the basics:

- **pwd (Print Working Directory):** Reveals your current position in the file system hierarchy.
- **ls (List):** Illuminates the files and directories within your current location. Can be customized with options like -l (long format) and -a (show hidden files)
- **cd (Change Directory):** The heart of navigation. Use it with absolute paths (e.g., cd /var/log) or relative paths (e.g., cd Documents/Projects)
- **.. (Parent Directory):** Your shortcut for moving one level upwards.

Mastering Relative Paths

Moving around using purely absolute paths can get cumbersome. Relative paths offer efficiency—they describe the route from where you are *now*. Here's how to craft them:

- **Single Dot .:** Represents your *current* directory. Not often used alone with cd, but it is helpful in other commands for referencing the current location.
- **Double Dots ..:** Represent the *parent* directory (one level above). Essential for moving upwards in the file system.
- **Directory Names:** Combine these to craft your path relative to your current position. For example, if you're in /home/yourusername, you could move into a 'Music' directory within it using cd Music.

The Power of ~ (Home Directory)

Your home directory acts as your base camp. The tilde symbol (~) is a magical shortcut that always represents it.

Examples:

- `cd ~`: Takes you back home, regardless of where you're roaming.
- `cd ~/Documents`: Jumps directly into your Documents directory.

Navigation Strategies

Let's apply these techniques in realistic scenarios:

Scenario 1: Quick Exploration You're in your home directory and want a peek inside the system's temporary directory:

1. `cd /tmp`
2. `ls` (Take a look around)
3. `cd ~` (Return instantly to your home directory)

Scenario 2: Structured Movement Your photos are scattered across various folders. You want to consolidate them into a 'Photos' directory within your home:

1. `cd ~` (Ensure you're in your home directory)
2. `mkdir Photos` (Create the destination directory)
3. `cd Downloads` (Assuming your photos are in Downloads)
4. `mv *.jpg ~/Photos/` (Move all .jpg files to the Photos directory)
5. Repeat step 4 as needed if you have photos in other locations

Pro Tips

- **Tab Completion:** Your best friend! Start typing a directory or filename, and press Tab to attempt auto-completion. This saves time and prevents errors due to typos.
- **"Up" and "Down" Arrow Keys:** Often, you just need to recall a previous command. The up and down arrow keys let you cycle through your command history – another huge time-saver!

Looking Ahead

This chapter gave you a strong foundation in precise navigation. Our adventure continues as we explore these concepts further:

- Advanced navigation for seamless movement across complex directory structures
- Precision tactics for pinpointing the files and directories you need, even in a crowded system
- **Discovering how to manipulate files and directories with powerful commands**

Additional Resources

- **Taming the Terminal:** A great, interactive set of Linux command-line tutorials https://linuxjourney.com/
- **Filenames and Paths in Linux:** A guide from the Linux Documentation Project: https://tldp.org/LDP/intro-linux/html/sect_03_01.html

Remember, practice is key! Open your terminal, navigate your own file system, and experiment to solidify your skills.

Charting Your Course Through Linux, Part 2: Advanced Techniques for Seamless Exploration

In this chapter, we'll venture beyond the basics, equipping you with techniques that will transform you from a cautious explorer to a fearless, efficient navigator.

Combining Techniques

The true power of the command line lies in combining simple commands—let's examine a few examples:

- **Finding and Moving Files:**
    1. `cd ~/Downloads`
    2. `mkdir Reports`
    3. `mv *.pdf Reports/` (Moves all PDF files into the new Reports directory)
- **Cleanup and Listing:**
    1. `rm *.tmp` (Deletes all files ending with ".tmp")
    2. `ls -l` (Shows a detailed listing to confirm the cleanup)

Mastering Path Construction

Often, you'll want to work on files located deep within your file system. Constructing accurate paths becomes crucial:

Scenario: A project named 'SuperProject' is nested several levels down within your Documents directory (`/home/yourusername/Documents/Projects/2024/ClientA/SuperProject`). You want to list all the text files inside it:

1. **Direct Approach:** `ls /home/yourusername/Documents/Projects/2024/ClientA/SuperProject/*.txt`
2. **Step-by-Step Approach:**

- ○ `cd /home/yourusername/Documents/Projects/2024/ClientA/SuperProject`
- ○ `ls *.txt`

3. **Leveraging the Power of ~:** `ls ~/Documents/Projects/2024/ClientA/SuperProject/*.txt`

Each strategy is viable! Choose the one that matches your thinking style.

The Importance of Directory Stack

Imagine your Linux terminal has a built-in stack of plates (a last-in, first-out structure). Two commands let you manipulate this stack:

- **pushd (Push Directory):** Adds a directory to the top of the stack and simultaneously 'cd's into it. Great for temporary detours. Example: `pushd ~/Documents/Reports`
- **popd (Pop Directory):** Takes you back to the directory that was at the top of the stack before the last `pushd`, removing that directory from the stack. It's like your "back" button for navigation.

Scenario: You're deep within a project directory, but need to quickly access a configuration file in `/etc`, then return to your exact location.

1. `pushd /etc`
2. (Do what you need to do in /etc)
3. `popd` (Instantly back to your previous project directory)

Advanced Tips

- **Recall Previous Directories:** Sometimes, you need to quickly go back to a directory you were in a few steps ago. Typing `cd -` does exactly that! It swaps your current and previous working directory.
- **sudo Power:** A word of caution! The `sudo` command grants you temporary administrative privileges. Use this power responsibly when navigating system directories, as incorrect actions can have consequences.

What's Coming Up

We've now built a robust foundation for advanced navigation. Prepare for the next chapter, where we'll unlock the secrets to pinpoint-precise file and directory selection for masterful command-line control.

Additional Resources

- **The Linux Command Handbook:** https://linuxcommand.org/
- **Advanced Bash Scripting Guide:** https://tldp.org/LDP/abs/html/ (While focused on scripting, this resource dives deep into advanced techniques)

Charting Your Course Through Linux, Part 3: Precision Navigation Strategies Unveiled

Let's continue our journey of navigational mastery with "Charting Your Course Through Linux, Part 3: Precision Navigation Strategies Unveiled." We'll arm you with laser-focused techniques for pinpointing the exact files and directories you need within the vast landscape of your Linux system.

The Power of Wildcards

Wildcards are special characters that let you match patterns within file and directory names. Let's introduce the core players:

- **Asterisk (*)** : Matches zero or more characters. This is your "match anything" tool.
  - Example: `ls report*.pdf` lists files like "report.pdf", "report_final.pdf", even "report_old_backup_2022.pdf"
- **Question Mark (?)** : Matches any single character. Great for substituting a single unknown letter or digit.
  - Example: `mv image??.jpg Backup/` moves files like "image01.jpg," "image15.jpg," but not "image001.jpg"

Practical Wildcard Applications

Let's translate these into real-world file management tasks:

1. **Task:** Delete all temporary files ending with `.tmp` within your Downloads directory.
   - **Solution:**
     - `cd ~/Downloads`
     - `rm *.tmp`
2. **Task:** List all files within your Documents that were modified specifically on March 20th of this year. (You don't recall the exact filenames). We'll need the output of the `date` command for this:
   - `modification_date=$(date +%Y-%m-20)`
   - `ls -l ~/Documents/?$modification_date*`

Caution: Wildcards, especially the asterisk (*), are potent! Always double-check your commands (perhaps using just `ls` first) before executing anything destructive like `rm`.

Combining Commands for Complex Searches

The true power of the command line lies in combining tools. Let's look at some advanced techniques:

1. **Finding Files by Type:** The `find` command offers granular file searching, far beyond what wildcards alone can do.
    - Example: `find ~/Documents -type f -name "*.txt"` (Searches for all text files within your Documents directory)
2. **Filtering Results:** The pipe (|) symbol lets you send the output of one command as input to another. Let's refine the above search:
    - `find ~/Documents -type f -name "*.txt" | grep "invoice"` (This would find text files within Documents and then further filter to only show those containing the word "invoice")

Beyond the Basics

We've now moved beyond simple navigation! Let's look at a concept that trips up many users—filenames with spaces and other special characters:

Important: To ensure the command line interprets a filename containing spaces or special characters as a *single entity*, you need to enclose it in quotes.

- **Incorrect:** `mv my presentation.odp Documents` (The command line will try to operate on "my" and "presentation.odp" as separate units)
- **Correct:** `mv "my presentation.odp" Documents`

Pro Tip: Tab completion is your lifesaver with complex filenames! Start typing and hit Tab to save time and avoid errors, especially when special characters are involved.

Journey Ahead

In our next chapter, we'll conclude our navigation saga by reaching a state of 'Navigational Mastery Unleashed.' We'll explore how to make the command-line even more intuitive and uncover hidden powers that streamline operations!

Additional Resources

- **Regular Expressions:** A deeper dive into pattern matching: https://www.regular-expressions.info/
- **The find Command:** Detailed explanation on Linux Handbook: https://linuxcommand.org/lc3_man_pages/find1.html

Remember, practice makes perfect. Create some test files and directories in a clearly marked section of your file system, and experiment fearlessly with the techniques from this chapter!

Charting Your Course Through Linux, Part 4: Navigational Mastery Unleashed

In this chapter, we'll solidify your skills and add a few expert tricks to transform you from a skilled navigator into a command-line virtuoso!

Customizing Your Prompt

The prompt in your terminal (often something like `username@hostname:~$`) is customizable! Modifying it can add valuable information and make navigation smoother.

- **Environment Variables:** Your Linux system stores configuration values in environment variables. Some interesting ones for your prompt:
    - PS1: Controls your primary prompt's appearance
    - USER: Your current username
    - HOSTNAME: The name of the machine you're on
    - PWD: Your current working directory

Tip: Before changing your prompt, store your current PS1 value in a temporary variable (e.g., `temp_prompt=$PS1`) so you can easily revert if needed.

Example Prompt Customization

Let's make a prompt that shows `[username @ hostname: Short_Directory_Path] $`. Here's how:

1. **Understanding Escape Sequences:** To format text within the prompt, special escape sequences are used. You'll need:
    - \u: Inserts your username
    - \h: Inserts your hostname
    - \W: Shows the last segment of your current directory
    - \$: Adds a regular '$' symbol for non-root users (or '#' if you're root)
2. **Setting the Prompt:**
    - `export PS1="[\u@\h: \W]\$ "`

Pro Tip: Put this `export PS1...` line in a special file called `.bashrc` in your home directory to make the change permanent across terminal sessions.

Power Shortcuts

Master these keyboard shortcuts to work seamlessly within your terminal:

- **Ctrl + A:** Jumps the cursor to the beginning of the command line
- **Ctrl + E:** Jumps the cursor to the end of the command line
- **Ctrl + U:** Clears the line from the cursor position to the beginning
- **Ctrl + K:** Clears the line from the cursor position to the end
- **Ctrl + L:** Clears the screen (same effect as the `clear` command)

Recall and Modify Previous Commands

No more retyping long commands! Let's explore ways to interact with your command history:

- **Up/Down Arrows:** Cycle through recent commands
- **Ctrl + R:** Initiates a reverse search. Start typing any part of a previous command, and it will search your history
- **`history`:** Lists your recent command history

Advanced History Magic

- **`!number`:** Executes a command from your history by its number (as seen using the `history` command)
- **`!!`:** Executes the very last command you ran
- **`!$`:** Replaces itself with the last argument from the previous command. Great for repeating an operation on a new file!

Scenario:

1. You list files with `ls -l /var/log/`
2. You want to use the `less` command to view the last file in that listing: `less /var/log/!$`

A Note on Shells

The specific way you customize prompts and some command-line behavior may vary slightly depending on your Linux distribution and the shell you're using (common ones are Bash, Zsh, and others).

Next Steps

Your navigational prowess is formidable! Our introduction to the command line ends here, but your journey continues. Ahead lie:

- **The secrets of file linking (both hard and soft links)**
- **Understanding and customizing the powerful "ls" command**
- **Managing files with precision**

Additional Resources

- **Explainshell.com:** Breaks down complex commands with clear explanations: https://explainshell.com/
- **Linux Shell Scripting Tutorial (Bash):** https://linuxconfig.org/bash-scripting-tutorial-for-beginners While focused on scripting, this dives deep into customization.

Unveiling File Secrets: Comprehensive Directory and File Listing Strategies

Get ready to uncover the hidden details and structures within your Linux file system with this chapter, "Unveiling File Secrets: Comprehensive Directory and File Listing Strategies." Think of this as going from simply seeing what's in a room to understanding the materials things are built from and the history behind them.

The Essential 'ls' Command

The foundation of revealing file and directory information lies in the ls command. Let's recap the basics and then dive deeper:

- ls: Lists files and directories in your current location.
- ls -l: Provides a long listing format including:
    - Permissions (e.g., rwxr-xr–)
    - Owner & Group
    - File Size
    - Modification Time/Date
- ls -a: Reveals hidden files and directories (names starting with '.')

Harnessing the Power of Options

Let's explore some commonly used options to customize how ls presents its output:

- **-h (Human Readable):** Displays file sizes in easier-to-read formats, like KB, MB, and GB.
- **-t:** Sorts the output by modification time, with the most recently modified files appearing first.
- **-R (Recursive):** Lists the contents of directories, their subdirectories, and so on. Essential for understanding the full structure of a location.
- **-S:** Sorts files and directories based on size, making it simple to spot your largest files.

Combining Options

The magic is in combining options! For example:

- `ls -lhrt` : Gives you a long format listing, human-readable file sizes, sorted with the most recently modified at the bottom.

Scenario: You suspect large files are filling up your home directory. To investigate:

1. `cd ~`
2. `ls -lSh` (This will show a size-based listing with the largest files on top)

Controlling the Depth of Recursion

When using the recursive `-R` option, you might want to limit how deep it goes. Here's how:

- **`--max-depth=N`:** Where 'N' is a number. This restricts the listing to 'N' levels down from your current location.

Example: `ls -R --max-depth=2` (Shows your current directory, its immediate subdirectories, and the contents of those subdirectories)

File and Directory Detail with 'stat'

While `ls` is powerful, sometimes you need a microscopic view of a file or directory. The `stat` command comes to the rescue:

- **`stat filename`** Provides in-depth information, including:
    - File type (regular file, directory, etc.)
    - Inode number (a unique identifier within the file system)
    - Access permissions
    - Multiple timestamps (creation, last modification, last access)

Pro Tip: The output of `stat` can be a bit overwhelming at first. Focus on the key sections like file type, permissions, and the various timestamps.

Beyond the Basics

We've now gone a big step further than simply viewing the contents of a directory. Let's look at some use cases where these techniques shine:

- **Troubleshooting Permissions:** If you can't access a file, the output of `ls -l` and `stat` can reveal why (e.g., incorrect permissions).

- **Identifying File Types:** Not sure what kind of file you're dealing with? The `file` command (which we'll cover in a later chapter) combined with `ls` can tell you definitively.
- **Auditing System Changes:** Want to know which files changed most recently on your system? A combination of `ls`, sorting, and potentially the `find` command can become your investigative tool.

Additional Resources

- **Linux Manual (man) Pages:** Search for `man ls` and `man stat` for the ultimate reference.
- **The Linux Documentation Project:** https://tldp.org/ (Provides excellent guides on commands and concepts).

Remember, practice is key! Create files, directories, experiment with permissions, and use these commands to dissect the results. The more you explore, the more comfortable you'll become with the inner workings of your Linux file system.

Linking the Unlinkable: Demystifying Hard vs. Soft Links

In the Linux world, links provide a powerful way to create multiple pathways to the same data, opening up incredible flexibility.

The Essence of a File

Before diving into links, let's solidify your understanding of what a file truly represents on a Linux system:

- **Inodes:** The heart of a file isn't just its name or the data it contains. Every file has an 'inode' – a unique data structure storing:
    - Metadata (permissions, ownership, timestamps, etc.)
    - Pointers to the actual blocks where the file's data resides on the disk.
- **Filenames:** The filenames you interact with are like convenient labels pointing to the underlying inode.

Introducing Links

A link in Linux is an alternative way to get to an existing file's inode. There are two fundamental types:

1. **Hard Links**
    - **The Indistinguishable Twin:** A hard link is like a second, equally valid name for an existing file. They both point to the *same inode*.
    - **Restrictions:**
        - Cannot be created for directories (for system stability reasons)
        - Can't span across different file systems (e.g., different partitions)
    - **Think of It Like:** Adding a second doorway into the same room.
2. **Soft Links (Also Called Symbolic Links)**
    - **The Clever Shortcut:** A soft link is a special kind of file that just contains a *path* to the original file (the target).
    - **Flexibility:** Can be created for both files and directories, and can even point to files on different file systems.
    - **Think of It Like:** A signpost saying, "The actual house is that way!"

Use Cases – Why Use Links?

- **Organization:** Create multiple access points to a file within your file system structure without duplicating the data.
- **Shared Libraries:** Programs often rely on shared libraries. Links ensure various programs can find the correct library versions.
- **Backups:** Some backup strategies utilize hard links to create 'snapshots' that appear as full files but take minimal extra space (until the originals change).
- **Flexibility for Programs:** Allow a program to find a resource using a standard path, even if the physical file location needs to change.

Let's See Links in Action (A word of caution: Exercise care when experimenting with link creation!)

Scenario 1: Hard Link

1. **Create a file:** `touch original_file.txt`
2. **Make a hard link:** `ln original_file.txt hard_link.txt`
3. **Observe:**
   - `ls -li` (Note the inode numbers of both files will be identical)
   - Modifying either `original_file.txt` or `hard_link.txt` changes the same underlying data!

Scenario 2: Soft Link

1. **Create a soft link:** `ln -s original_file.txt soft_link.txt`
2. **Observe:**
   - `ls -li` (The soft link has a different inode, and shows an '->' indicating its target)
   - Editing `soft_link.txt` won't truly modify it; it may edit the 'original_file.txt' if it still exists.
   - Deleting `original_file.txt` leaves a 'broken' soft link pointing nowhere.

Next Steps We've unveiled the core concepts of hard and soft links. Get ready to explore:

- Commands to create and manage different types of links.
- Advanced applications of links and how they streamline complex file structures.

Additional Resources

- **Hard Links and Soft Links:** A clear explanation on GeeksforGeeks: https://www.geeksforgeeks.org/hard-links-soft-links-unixlinux/
- **The Linux Documentation Project:** https://tldp.org/ (Offers in-depth guides on commands and concepts)

Crafting Linux Links, Part 1: Initiating Link Creation Techniques

Let's dive into the practical side of links with "Crafting Linux Links, Part 1: Initiating Link Creation Techniques." In this chapter, we'll turn the concepts of hard and soft links into tools you can wield with power and precision.

Harnessing the 'ln' Command

The `ln` command is your gateway to forging links:

- **Basic Syntax:** `ln [options] target link_name`

Let's break it down:

- **options:** Modifiers to control the type of link created (we'll get to these soon)
- **target:** The existing file or directory you want to link to.
- **link_name:** The name of the new link you're creating.

The Art of the Hard Link

1. **Command:** `ln target_file hard_link_file`
   - **Important:** You cannot hard link directories!
2. **Verification:**
   - `ls -li target_file hard_link_file` Observe the identical inode numbers
   - Modify one of the files, and use `ls` or a text editor to confirm both have changed.

Example Scenario: You're working on an important presentation, 'report.odp', and want another access point within your 'Documents' directory:

1. `cd ~/Documents`
2. `ln ../report.odp presentation_report.odp` (Assuming the original is one level outside Documents)

Mastering the Symbolic (Soft) Link

1. **Command:** `ln -s target_file_or_directory soft_link_name`
   - The crucial option here is `-s`.
2. **Verification:**
   - `ls -l soft_link_name` You'll see the '->' indicator in the output

Example Scenario: Your music collection is on an external drive, and you want to easily access it from within your '~/Music' directory:

1. `ln -s /media/usbdisk/Music_Collection ~/Music/External_Music` (Adjust the paths according to your system)

Caution: Broken Links

- Soft links are susceptible to breakage. If the original target is deleted or moved, the soft link is left pointing to a non-existent location.
- Commands and scripts that rely on the soft link may then fail.

Common Options for the 'ln' Command

- **-f (Force):** Overwrites an existing link if the `link_name` is already used. Use with care!
- **-i (Interactive):** Prompts you before overwriting any existing files.
- **-v (Verbose):** Provides more descriptive output, helpful for understanding what is happening.

Tips

- **Relative vs. Absolute Paths:** You can use either when creating links. Relative paths are often more flexible if you anticipate moving directory structures around.
- **Tab Completion Is Your Friend:** Especially for long path names, let your terminal help!

What's Next?

We've begun our link creation journey. Upcoming, prepare to explore:

- More advanced scenarios for link usage
- Strategies for managing and resolving broken links

- Delving deeper into the subtle differences and powers of hard and soft links

Additional References

- **Linux Manual (man pages):** Run man ln for the definitive reference.
- **Explainshell.com:** Breaks down complex commands with clear examples: https://explainshell.com/

Important: I highly recommend creating a clearly-named "test" directory within your home directory to experiment with link creation.

Crafting Linux Links, Part 2: Advanced Linking Strategies Revealed

Get ready to take your link mastery to the next level and learn how to restructure directories and handle complex scenarios with finesse.

Refresher: Key Points from Part 1

- **Hard Links:** Multiple names for the same file (same inode). Changes to one are reflected in the other.
- **Soft Links:** Like shortcuts; point to a target file or directory. If the target is moved or deleted, the soft link may break.
- **The `ln` Command:** Your link-crafting toolbox.

Advanced Use Cases

Let's explore some scenarios where links offer elegant solutions:

Scenario 1: Organizing Across File Systems

You have a large project that spans your main hard drive and an external backup drive. To keep things organized, you want a 'Project' folder in your home directory that seamlessly accesses files in both locations without duplication.

1. **Create Structure on External Drive:**
   - Let's assume the external drive mounts at `/media/backupdrive`
   - `mkdir /media/backupdrive/Project`
2. **Selective Hard Linking:**
   - `cd ~/Project` (Create a 'Project' folder in your home directory)
   - `ln /media/backupdrive/Project/important_document.txt .` (Hard link the specific document) Repeat the hard linking process for other essential files.

Result: Your 'Project' folder now has a mix of regular files (perhaps created directly within it) and hard links. No wasted space, and everything is accessible in one place!

Scenario 2: Restructuring After the Fact

You've been working on a set of scripts, but they've become disorganized. A program expects them in `/usr/local/bin/myscripts`. Moving them would break other tools that rely on their existing location.

1. **Create the Target Directory:**
   - `sudo mkdir /usr/local/bin/myscripts` (We'll likely need `sudo` permissions for this area).
2. **Craft Soft Links:**
   - `cd` to your existing script directory.
   - `ln -s $(pwd)/* /usr/local/bin/myscripts` (This creates soft links in the target directory to all items in the current directory).

Result: Your program finds the scripts where it expects, and your other tools keep working, thanks to the resilient nature of soft links!

Managing Broken Links

- **Finding Broken Links:** The `find` command is powerful for this:
   - `find /path/to/start -xtype l` (`-xtype l` specifically searches for broken links)
- **Dealing with Broken Links:**
   - **Option 1: Recreate the Link:** If the original target still exists in a new location, update the soft link to point to it.
   - **Option 2: Remove the Link:** Use `rm broken_link_name`.

Special Considerations

- **Recursive Linking (-r option):** The `ln` command can recursively link directories, but this is rarely needed and must be used with extreme caution! A mistake could intertwine your file system in unintended ways.
- **Version Control & Links:** Most version control systems (like Git) don't track soft links effectively by default. Special handling might be needed to ensure links are preserved.

Parting Thoughts

Understanding the nuances of hard and soft links allows you to reimagine the way you organize files on your Linux system. They provide flexibility that simple copying cannot match.

What's Ahead

In future chapters, we'll look at harnessing links to create dynamic workspaces and learn to integrate them seamlessly into your workflows.

Additional Resources

- **GNU.org ln documentation:** The official details:
  https://www.gnu.org/software/coreutils/manual/html_node/ln-invocation.html
- **Soft Links vs. Hard Links Article:** Clear explanations on GeeksforGeeks:
  https://www.geeksforgeeks.org/hard-links-soft-links-unixlinux/

Looping in Linux: Harnessing the Power of Soft Links for Dynamic Directory Structures

Get ready to reshape your understanding of directory organization with "Looping in Linux: Harnessing the Power of Soft Links for Dynamic Directory Structures." In this chapter, we'll see how soft links enable you to create flexible structures that adapt to your changing workflows effortlessly.

A Quick Recap: The Magic of Soft Links

- They act as sophisticated pointers to a target file or directory.
- Deleting a soft link doesn't affect the target.
- Moving or renaming the target leads to a "broken" link, which might be desirable in some scenarios.

Scenario 1: The Evolving Project

You're collaborating on a project with multiple stages – development, testing, and release. Each stage might prefer slightly different file arrangements.

1. **Base Structure:**
   - `/projects/SuperProject/src` (Source code)
   - `/projects/SuperProject/data` (Test data)
2. **Stage-Specific Views with Links:**
   - **Development:**
     - `mkdir /projects/SuperProject/dev`
     - `ln -s ../src /projects/SuperProject/dev/`
     - `ln -s ../data /projects/SuperProject/dev/input_data` (Rename link for clarity)
   - **Testing**
     - `mkdir /projects/SuperProject/testing`
     - `ln -s ../src /projects/SuperProject/testing/code_under_test`
     - `ln -s ../data /projects/SuperProject/testing/`

Benefits

- **Customization:** Each stage has its own workspace without file duplication.
- **Centralized Source:** Changes in the 'src' or 'data' folders propagate to all linked views.
- **Flexibility:** If project structure changes, only the base needs adjustment; the links remap automatically.

Scenario 2: Application Versioning

You manage software with multiple installed versions. A 'current' link ensures the right version is always activated.

1. **Versioned Installations**
   - `/usr/local/myapp-1.0`
   - `/usr/local/myapp-2.0`
2. **The 'Current' Link**
   - `sudo ln -s /usr/local/myapp-2.0 /usr/local/myapp-current`
3. **Updating**
   - Install new versions (e.g., `/usr/local/myapp-2.1`).
   - Change the link target:
     `sudo ln -sfn /usr/local/myapp-2.1 /usr/local/myapp-current` (The `-f` forces overwriting and `-n` treats the link name as a normal file, important for updating!)

Benefits

- **Seamless Switching:** Scripts relying on `/usr/local/myapp-current` always use the designated version.
- **Quick Rollback:** If an update causes issues, repoint the link to an older version instantly.

Cautions & Best Practices

- **Circular Links:** Avoid linking directories in a way that creates a loop (where a directory ends up linked within itself). This confuses most commands and can lead to trouble.
- **Clarity of Purpose:** If you have many links, good naming is crucial to keep track of why they exist.

- **Broken Links:** Be prepared to monitor for broken links, especially in dynamic setups like the versioning example above.

Advanced Use Case: User-Centric Home Directories

Imagine customizing the home directory experience for different users based on their roles within an organization:

- **Base Structure:**
    - `/home/shared/applications`
    - `/home/shared/documents/standard_templates`
- **User 'developer1':**
    - `ln -s /home/shared/applications ~/Applications`
    - `ln -s /home/shared/documents/standard_templates/dev_report.odp ~/Templates`
- **User 'accountant2':**
    - `ln -s /home/shared/applications ~/CompanyApps`
    - `ln -s /home/shared/documents/standard_templates/budget.ods ~/Templates`

Power of the Approach

- Centralized, easy to update resources for your organization.
- Users get a tailored experience immediately upon login.

Let's Get Practical

Think about how your own work could benefit from dynamic directory structures. Do you have projects with multiple components? Do you install software that needs careful management? Outline an example!

Next Up

We'll start delving into the `ls` command's power and finesse to get a truly accurate view of your file system, empowering your organization.

Additional Resources

- **Linux Documentation Project on Symbolic Links:** https://tldp.org/

Unveiling the Array of Options: Exploring Enhanced Functionality of the `ls` Command, Part 1

Get ready to transform your understanding of file listings with "Unveiling the Array of Options: Exploring Enhanced Functionality of the `ls` Command, Part 1." Think of this as going from viewing a basic directory list to having an X-ray machine that reveals hidden details within your file system.

The Power of Versatility

The `ls` command, a cornerstone of command-line navigation, is far mightier than it might initially seem. Let's start our deep dive by controlling the information it presents.

Key Options: The Basics

You likely are familiar with some of these, but we'll use them as a foundation:

- **-l (long format):** Provides a wealth of information, including:
  - File permissions
  - Ownership (user and group)
  - File size
  - Modification timestamps
  - Number of hard links (if any)
- **-a (all files):** Includes hidden files (those starting with a `.`)
- **-h (human-readable sizes):** Displays file sizes in KB, MB, GB for easier interpretation.

Combining Options

The real power comes when you combine these. `ls -lah` is a very common starting point for getting a detailed, human-friendly directory listing.

Scenario 1: Permission Troubleshooting

You're trying to run a script, but it fails with a 'permission denied' error.

1. **Start with the Basics:** `cd` to the directory containing the script.
2. **Get the Details:** `ls -l script_name.sh`

- ○ Focus on the very first part of the output, which looks like `-rw-r--r--`. This tells you:
    - **File Type:** The leading – means regular file.
    - **Owner Permissions:** The next 'rw-' means **R**ead, **W**rite, but no e**X**ecute for the owner.
    - **Group Permissions:** 'r–' means the group has **R**ead only.
    - **Other Permissions:** 'r–' means others (anyone else) have **R**ead only.

Note: To *change* permissions, you would need the chmod command, which warrants its own chapter!

Scenario 2: Spotting Large Files

Your disk is getting full. You need a quick way to identify the largest files in your home directory:

1. **List Everything:** `ls -lah ~`
2. **Sort by Size:** `ls -lah ~ | sort -rh -k5`
    - ○ We're introducing 'piping' here, where the output of `ls` is fed into the `sort` command. Detail on piping will come later! The key part is `-rh -k5`, which tells `sort` to do a reverse (largest to smallest), human-readable sort based on the 5th column (file size).

Going Deeper

Let's introduce a few more powerful options, with practical examples to come:

- **-S (Sort by Size):** Does what it says on the tin – directly sorts the `ls` output by file size.
- **-t (Sort by time):** Orders your listing with the most recently modified at the top.
- **-d (Directories only):** When used along with `-l`, it shows information about the directory itself rather than its contents.
- **-R (Recursive):** We've used this before, but its power comes through when combined with other options for detailed listings of entire directory trees.

Practice Time!

Create a 'test' directory within your home directory. Populate it with:

- A few regular files (use the `touch` command if needed)
- Some hidden files (create names starting with `.`)
- A subdirectory or two

Now experiment! Try these:

- `ls -a` vs. `ls -al`
- `ls -t` vs `ls -lt`
- `ls -lSr`

Observe the differences!

Next Up

In the coming parts of this series on `ls`, we'll learn to:

- Filter listings to show only specific file types or names
- Master the display of timestamps
- Dive into more advanced sorting techniques

Additional Resources

- **The Linux man page for ls:** Run `man ls` at your terminal for the definitive reference.
- **Explainshell.com:** Breaks down `ls` options along with many other commands: https://explainshell.com/

Unveiling the Array of Options: Exploring Enhanced Functionality of the `ls` Command, Part 2

Let's continue our deep dive into the power of the `ls` command with "Unveiling the Array of Options: Exploring Enhanced Functionality of the `ls` Command, Part 2." This time, we'll focus on filtering, fine-tuning timestamps, and mastering advanced sorting techniques.

Filtering for Focused Listings

Often, you don't want to see *everything* in a directory. Let's learn to narrow down our `ls` output:

1. **By File Type:**
    - `ls -l *.txt` : Lists text files (ending in .txt)
    - `ls -l -d */` Lists directories only (useful when there are many files cluttering the view)
2. **Pattern Matching with Wildcards:**
    - `ls -l project_2022*` Lists files or directories starting with "project_2022"
    - `ls -l *backup*` Lists anything with "backup" anywhere in its name.

Scenario: Image Management

You have a folder '~/Pictures' filled with photos, but also some random documents that got mixed in:

- `ls -l ~/Pictures/*.jpg` Gives a clean list of your JPEG images.
- `ls -l ~/Pictures/*` (List everything)
    - Follow this up with `mv *.pdf ~/Documents` to relocate any stray PDFs.

Timestamp Control

The `-l` option gives us modification time, but there's more to uncover:

- **-c:** Shows when the file's *inode* was last changed (this includes metadata changes like permissions, not just content edits)
- **-u:** Displays the file's last *access* time.
- **--full-time:** Provides full date and time information with seconds precision.

Scenario: Tracking Changes

You suspect a configuration file is being edited unexpectedly. Let's investigate:

1. `ls -l /etc/important_config.conf` (Get a baseline)
2. Wait a while...
3. `ls -lc /etc/important_config.conf` Compare with the previous output - a changed 'c' timestamp might indicate tampering!

Advanced Sorting

Let's go beyond the basics of sorting by size (`-S`) or modification time (`-t`) :

- **-v (Version Sorting):** Intelligently sorts names that contain numbers, placing "document-10.odp" after "document-2.odp" (which wouldn't happen with a basic string sort).
- **-X (Sort by Extension):** Groups files with the same extensions together within the listing.

Scenario: Cleaning Up Downloads

Your 'Downloads' folder is a mess. Get some order:

1. `cd ~/Downloads`
2. `ls -lX` Files are now grouped by type (ZIP, DMG, etc.), making it easier to spot what you might want to clean out.

Combining for Ultimate Control

The true magic of `ls` comes from combining these techniques. Let's look at a complex but practical example:

`ls -ltra --full-time *.zip *.tar.gz`

- **-ltra :** Long format, sorted by last access time in reverse order (most recent at the bottom for ease of review).

- `--full-time`: Detailed timestamps for precision
- `*.zip *.tar.gz`: Limits output to ZIP and compressed TAR archives

Practice Time

Using the test directory you might have created from Part 1 of this `ls` exploration:

- List only hidden files that have been modified within the last 24 hours.
- Get a long listing of all files ending in '.jpg', sorted by their access time (most recently accessed at the top).
- Experiment with `-X`, `-v`, and try combinations!

Up Next

We still have much to cover about the `ls` command, including:

- Customizing the output format for very specific information needs.
- Integration with other commands for powerful file operations based on listings.

Additional Resources

- **GNU Documentation on ls:** Slightly less user-friendly than man `ls`, but offers some deeper details: https://www.gnu.org/software/coreutils/ls

Unveiling the Array of Options: Exploring Enhanced Functionality of the `ls` Command, Part 3

This time, let's go beyond standard listings and learn to make `ls` output information tailored precisely to our investigative needs.

Customizing the Output Format

The `--format` option gives you incredible control over what information `ls` displays *and* how it arranges it:

- **Presets:**
    - `--format=long` or `-l`: Our familiar friend!
    - `--format=commas` or `-m`: Comma-separated names – great for copying into other commands.
    - `--format=horizontal` or `-x`: Displays names across the screen.
    - `--format=vertical` or `-1`: Single column listing (filenames only)

Custom Specifiers

Let's build a custom format. Imagine we need: File Size, Owner, Modification Month-Day, Filename. Here's the command:

```
ls --format=single-column -l --time-style="+%b %d" %s %u %n
```

- This looks complex, but let's break it down:
    - `--format=single-column`: Ensures one file per line
    - `-l`: We still want the detail of a long listing
    - `--time-style="+%b %d"`: Modifies the date to show Month and Day only
    - `%s %u %n`: Specifiers for File Size, Owner Username, Filename

Scenario: Audit for Large Files

You need to find the biggest space hogs owned by a specific user ('bigdatauser'):

1. **Adapt the Custom Format:**

```
ls --format=single-column -l --time-style="+%b %d" %s
%u %n /home/bigdatauser
```

2. **Sort the Output:** Often, you'll want to feed this into the sort command:

```
ls -format=single-column -l --time-style="+%b %d" %s
%u %n /home/bigdatauser | sort -rn
``       (`-rn` tells `sort` to do a reverse numeric
sort)
```

The Power of `--group-directories-first`

While not strictly about formatting, it's incredibly useful when mixed with custom outputs. It forces `ls` to list all directories at the top before showing files, giving a visual break in your results.

Almost Like a Spreadsheet

By carefully crafting our `--format` specifiers, we can make `ls` output resemble a simple spreadsheet, excellent for analysis or feeding into other tools!

Controlling Information Density

Let's introduce a few more handy options:

- **`--block-size=SIZE`:** Forces size displays using a specific unit. Examples: `--block-size=KB`, `--block-size=M` (Note: this can cause some odd rounding in the output)
- **`--quoting-style=WORD`:** Controls how filenames that contain special characters are displayed. Useful values are:
  - `literal` : No quoting

- `shell` : Quotes in a way suitable for copying back into a shell command
- `escape`: Escapes non-printable characters

Scenario: Handling Filenames with Spaces

1. `ls -l` (Normal output - filenames with spaces might be hard to interpret)
2. `ls -l --quoting-style=shell` (Now, those filenames are in single quotes, unambiguous even for other commands)

Practice Makes Perfect

Remember your 'test' directory! Try these challenges:

- Create a listing showing only file permissions, owner, group, and filename.
- List all files in a directory, including hidden ones, sorted with directories grouped at the top, showing modification year and size in megabytes.
- Get a comma-separated list of just the filenames, with any special characters escaped.

What's Next

There's still a bit more `ls` power left to uncover, including how to integrate it seamlessly with other commands for streamlined file management workflows.

Additional Resources

- **GNU ls documentation:** The nitty-gritty details, if you need to go very deep: https://www.gnu.org/software/coreutils/ls

Unveiling the Array of Options: Exploring Enhanced Functionality of the `ls` Command, Part 4

Let's embark on the final chapter of our in-depth `ls` exploration with "Unveiling the Array of Options: Exploring Enhanced Functionality of the `ls` Command, Part 4." This time, we focus on integrating `ls` with other commands for powerful workflows and squeezing even more information out of those file listings.

Pipelines: The Power of Command Chains

In Linux, the output of one command can become the input to another. This is done through 'pipes', represented by the | symbol. Let's see how this supercharges `ls`:

Scenario 1: Focusing on a File Type

You only care about image files in your current directory:

1. `ls -l` (Too much information!)
2. `ls -l | grep ".jpg"` (The output of `ls` is piped into `grep`, which searches for lines containing ".jpg")

Scenario 2: Counting Results

How many text files are in your Documents folder?

`ls -l ~/Documents/*.txt | wc -l` (The `wc -l` command counts lines)

Important: The order of commands in a pipeline matters!

Beyond `grep`: More Useful Pipe Partners

- **sort:** We've seen this already. Sort the output of `ls` based on various criteria.
- **head and tail:** Extract only the beginning or end of the `ls` results, great for limiting large listings.

- **more or less:** If your `ls` output would normally overflow the screen, pipe it into a 'pager' like `less` for controlled scrolling.

Complex Example: Investigating Large Files

Let's chain several ideas together:

```
ls -lSr /home/my_username/ | head -n 10 | awk '{print $5, $9}'
```

1. `ls -lSr`: Detailed listing, largest files first, targetting your home directory.
2. `head -n 10`: Extract only the top 10 results (preventing screen overflow).
3. `awk '{print $5, $9}'`: awk does in-line text manipulation, here grabbing just the 5th and 9th columns (size and filename)

The -1 Option (One File Per Line)

Remember the `-1` option for `ls`? This forces one filename per line. It's **essential** if you plan to pipe `ls` output into another command that expects each 'line' to represent a single file.

Indirect File Operations with `xargs`

Let's say you want to delete all backup files (ending in `.bak`) in a directory. Here's how:

1. **First, test for safety!**
   - `ls -1 *.bak | xargs echo` (This would echo the filenames, letting you verify)
2. **Proceed with Deletion:**
   - `ls -1 *.bak | xargs rm` (Replaces 'echo' with 'rm')

Explanation: `xargs` takes input (in our case, the output of `ls`) and builds it into a command line fed to another program. **Caution:** `xargs` with `rm` can be dangerous! Always test first like we did above.

Finding the Right Information

Sometimes, the standard `ls` information isn't enough. Luckily, some less-commonly-used options exist:

- **`--file-type`:** Appends a character to each listing indicating the file type (/, *, @ for directory, executable, link, etc.)
- **`-i` (Inode numbers):** Lists the unique inode number of each file. Useful in some advanced scenarios.
- **`-F`:** Similar to `--file-type` but with slightly different indicators.

Scenario: Executable Hunting

Sometimes you need to find which files in a directory are directly executable:

`ls -lF | grep '\*$'` (We use `grep` here to find lines ending in a '*' character)

Next Steps (Going Further)

The world of command-line file management is vast. Our `ls` mastery unlocks powerful combination with tools like:

- **`find`:** Incredibly flexible search command for complex file finding scenarios.
- **Text Processing Power:** `sed`, `awk` for complex filtering and restructuring of `ls` output.

Additional Resources

- **Linux Pipelines Tutorial:** https://linuxize.com/post/linux-pipe-command/
- **xargs Explained:** https://linuxize.com/post/linux-xargs-command/

Practice Time

Using your 'test' directory, try these:

- List only the subdirectories, sorted by their last accessed time.
- Find all files modified in the last 24 hours, then get a count of those files.
- Experiment with combining the `--file-type` or `-i` options with other `ls` techniques we've learned.

Section 2:
Mastering File Operations

Time Travel with Files: Harnessing the Touch Command for Timestamp Mastery, Part 1

Get ready to bend time to your will! Let's dive into "Time Travel with Files: Harnessing the Touch Command for Timestamp Mastery, Part 1." The humble `touch` command is far more than it appears and crucial for precise file management.

The Basics

At its core, the purpose of `touch` is:

- **File Creation:** If a file doesn't exist, `touch filename` brings it into being as an empty file.
- **Timestamp Updating:** If the file *does* exist, `touch` modifies its access and modification timestamps to the current moment.

Scenario 1: Marking Progress

You're working on a long project with files like 'draft.txt', 'review.txt', 'final_version.txt'.

1. `touch review.txt` – If it doesn't exist, it's created. If it does, the timestamp signifies when you moved to the review stage.
2. Later, an `ls -lt` will clearly show the sequence you progressed through the files.

Key Options

Let's gain more control over our time travel:

- **-a (Access time only):** Updates only the file's "last accessed" timestamp.
- **-m (Modification time only):** Updates only the "last modified" timestamp.
- **-t (Specific time):** Lets you set a completely custom timestamp using the format `[[CC]YY]MMDDhhmm[.ss]`.
  - Example: `touch -t 202212201530.45 old_report.txt` (Sets the timestamp to Dec 20th, 2022 at 3:30 PM and 45 seconds)

Scenario 2: "As-Of" Backups

You need a snapshot of your source code folder *as it existed* last week.

1. **Create a Destination:** `mkdir project_backup_20231115`
2. **Selective Copying:** `cp project_source/*.java project_backup_20231115` (Copies over the code files)
3. **Time Travel:**
   - `cd project_backup_20231115`
   - `touch -t 202311150000 *.java` (Sets the timestamp of all Java files back to Nov 15th, 2023 at midnight)

Beyond the Current Time

You can use `touch -t` to set timestamps in the past (as we just did) or even in the future! This has some interesting niche uses, particularly in testing scenarios.

Cautions

- **touch Can Be Destructive:** If you mistype a filename while intending to update timestamps, you'll create a new empty file instead, overwriting the original!
- **Version Control Provides History:** For anything critical, a proper version control system like Git is the safer way to track changes over time.

Advanced Use Case: Triggering Automation

Some systems watch for files with recently updated timestamps to initiate actions. Example:

1. A program dumps data into 'new_data.csv' every hour.
2. A separate script is triggered on any change to 'new_data.csv' to process it.
3. You can use `touch new_data.csv` to manually force that script to run, even if the data hasn't actually changed.

File Systems Matter!

Not all file systems store timestamps with high precision. If you need accuracy down to the second, be sure your system supports it.

What's Next?

In Part 2, we'll combine `touch` with other commands to create sophisticated timestamp-based workflows and learn about file time restoration tools.

Additional Resources

- **Linux touch Manual (`man touch`):** The definitive source of information: https://www.gnu.org/software/coreutils/manual/html_node/touch-invocation.html
- **Example-filled touch explanation:** https://linuxize.com/post/how-to-use-the-touch-command-in-linux/

Practice Time

1. Create an empty file named 'reminder.txt'. Set its modification time to exactly two days from now.
2. Have a folder with several documents of different types. Use `touch` in a way that, after executing your command, an `ls -t` shows them ordered with the oldest at the top.

Time Travel with Files: Harnessing the Touch Command for Timestamp Mastery, Part 2

Let's go deeper, combining `touch` with other commands and exploring specialized timestamp tools.

Using touch with File Searches

The `find` command offers incredibly flexible file searches. We can integrate `touch` for timestamp adjustments on the results:

Scenario: Last Week's Work

Find all Python files in your project modified in the last 7 days, then 'refresh' them as if they were just edited.

1. **Search:** `find /path/to/project -name '*.py' -mtime -7` (Let's break this down:
   - `/path/to/project`: Where to start the search
   - `-name '*.py'`: Look for Python files
   - `-mtime -7`: Modified Time within the last 7 days)
2. **Time Travel:** `find /path/to/project -name '*.py' -mtime -7 -exec touch {} \;` (Key addition: `-exec touch {} \;`: This tells `find` to execute `touch` on each file found, the '{}' stands for the filename.)

Reference Files

Sometimes you need timestamps based on another file's time:

- **-r (Reference):** `touch -r reference_file target_file` This sets the timestamps of `target_file` to match those of `reference_file`.

Scenario: Aligning Backups

You update 'report.xlsx' and then generate a PDF copy 'report.pdf'. To make your backup tool treat them as changed together:

```
touch -r report.xlsx report.pdf
```

Advanced: Restoring Timestamps

Let's say you accidentally overwrote a file and have a backup, but it's slightly out of date. Can you rescue the *timestamps* from the old version, even if the content is wrong?

Some specialized tools help:

- `stat`: Displays detailed file information, including timestamps
- **File Systems Matter:** Not all file systems preserve this metadata perfectly or in ways easily accessible to users.

Example Workflow (Conceptual)

1. **Isolating Timestamps:** `stat backup_copy.txt > timestamp_info.txt` (Save timestamps from backup into a text file)
2. **Restoring Content:** Overwrite your current file with the 'correct' but outdated backup.
3. **Manipulation:** (This is where it gets system-specific). It might involve writing a small script to parse `timestamp_info.txt` and use the `touch -t` option to reapply the old timestamps.

Caution: This is an area where version control (like Git) is a far safer solution!

Command Chaining for Workflows

Let's build more elaborate examples using pipes ('|') to link commands:

Scenario: Sorting Files into Timestamped Folders

1. **Create Destination Folders:**
   - `mkdir 2023-11-16`
   - `mkdir 2023-11-17` (One for today, and yesterday)
2. **Find and Touch:**
   - `find . -maxdepth 1 -type f -mtime 1 -exec touch {} \;` (Finds files in the current directory modified in the last day, updates timestamps)
3. **Sorting Move:**
   - `find . -maxdepth 1 -type f -newermt 2023-11-16 -not -newermt 2023-11-17 -exec mv {} 2023-11-16`

        `\;` (Complex, but finds files whose timestamp falls within yesterday's date and moves them)

    ○ Repeat the `find...mv` line for today's folder

Practice Makes Perfect

Using your 'test' directory:

1. Set the timestamp of all '*.txt' files to a specific time in the future.
2. Create several empty files, then write a command-line sequence that uses `find`, `touch`, and `mv` to arrange those files into folders named 'Today' and 'Older'.

Resources

- **Linux find manual (`man find`):** Enormous number of options to explore:
  https://www.gnu.org/software/findutils/manual/html_node/find_html/index.html
- **touch and `stat` Examples on nixCraft:**
  https://www.cyberciti.biz/faq/linux-unix-appleosx-bsd-touch-command-examples/,
  https://www.cyberciti.biz/faq/linux-unix-stat-command-examples/

Building and Clearing Pathways: Exploring mkdir and rmdir for Directory Management

Get ready to become an architect of your Linux file system! These commands, while seemingly simple, are at the heart of organization.

mkdir: Foundations of Structure

The `mkdir` command is your tool for creating directories (folders).

Basic Use:

- `mkdir new_project` Creates a directory named 'new_project' in the current location.

Key Options:

- **-p (Parents):** Create any necessary parent directories.
  - Example: `mkdir -p project/2023/reports` creates the entire structure, even if 'project' and '2023' don't exist yet.
- **-v (Verbose):** Prints information about each directory created. Useful for confirming actions.

Scenario 1: Organized Photos

You want to sort your photos:

1. `mkdir Photos` (Base directory)
2. `mkdir -p Photos/Vacations/2022`
3. `mkdir -p Photos/Family/Portraits`

Scenario 2: Website Structure

You're setting up a simple website locally:

```
mkdir -p my_website/css
 mkdir my_website/images
mkdir my_website/js
```

rmdir: Clearing the Path

The `rmdir` command is the counterpart to `mkdir`, removing directories. **Important:** It only works on *empty* directories.

Basic Use:

- `rmdir old_reports` (Deletes the 'old_reports' directory)

Cautions

- `rmdir` is unforgiving! There's usually no "Trash" or "Recycle Bin" concept like in a graphical desktop.
- To delete a directory along with files inside it, you'll need the powerful (and dangerous!) `rm` command, which we'll cover in a future chapter.

Key Options

- **-p (Parents):** Also removes parent directories if they become empty. Example: `rmdir -p project/2023/reports` might also delete '2023' and 'project' if nothing else exists inside them.
- **-v (Verbose):** Explains what's being removed.

Scenario: Cleaning Up

1. Files from 'old_reports' have been moved elsewhere.
2. `rmdir -pv old_reports` would delete the directory and show you if this also removed parent directories due to them being empty.

Combining for Efficiency

Let's create and then remove a temporary work area:

```
mkdir project_workspace
# ... do work inside 'project_workspace' ...
rmdir -p project_workspace
```

Safety First: The Power of -i

Both `mkdir` and `rmdir` support a `-i` (interactive) option. This makes them ask for confirmation before each creation or deletion, acting as a safety net. Great for beginners!

Permissions: The Hidden Factor

Sometimes, you can't create or remove a directory even if it seems empty. This is due to file permissions. We'll cover those in more depth later, but be aware they exist!

Beyond the Basics

Let's get a bit more advanced:

- **Creating Numbered Sequences:** Using the command `seq -w 1 10` to generate numbers and a `for` loop (which we'll learn soon) we can do:

```
for i in $(seq -w 1 10); do mkdir folder_$i; done
```

- **Complex Removals:** The `rm -rf` command (covered later) can forcibly delete non-empty directories. *Handle with extreme care!*

Practice Time

1. Design a directory structure to organize your music collection by genre and year. Use the `mkdir -p` command to bring it into existence.
2. Create a "test_area" directory, create some sub-directories inside it, then safely practice using `rmdir` with the `-i` and `-v` options for interactivity and feedback.

Resources

- `mkdir` man page: (man mkdir)
- `rmdir` man page: (man rmdir)
- **Directory Management on ExplainShell.com:**
  https://explainshell.com/

Up Next

Now that we can build structures, the next challenge is to get rid of files safely and effectively. We'll delve into the `rm` command and its potential for both precision and destruction!

Removing Files Unleashed: Commanding the rm for Total File Annihilation, Part 1

Get ready to wield the destructive power of the `rm` command! In "Removing Files Unleashed: Commanding the rm for Total File Annihilation, Part 1" we'll learn the basics of file removal, how to use `rm` safely, and the crucial options that offer lifelines before it's too late.

Understanding the Stakes

Unlike deleting files in a graphical environment (where there's often a "Recycle Bin"), rm is generally permanent. Respect its power!

The Basics

- `rm filename`: Deletes the specified file.
- `rm file1 file2 file3`: Deletes multiple files.
- **Wildcards!**: Be cautious, as `rm *.txt` would delete *all* files ending in .txt in the current directory. We'll cover wildcards in detail later.

Key Options: Safety Nets & Force

- `-i` **(Interactive):** Prompts you with a "y/n" confirmation before deleting each file. Great for beginners!
- `-f` **(Force):** The opposite of `-i`. Deletes without asking, even if files are write-protected. *Use with extreme caution!*

Scenario 1: Careful Cleanup

You have several old log files (old_log.1, old_log.2, etc.)

1. `rm -i old_log.*` (Gives you a chance to review each deletion).

Scenario 2: Spring Cleaning

You're *confident* you want to nuke a whole directory full of temporary files:

1. `cd temp_files` (Important: Navigate INTO the directory)

2. `rm -rf *` (`-r` for recursive will delete the directory itself along with its contents)

Danger Zones

Let's explore why `rm` should be handled with care:

- **No Second Chances:** In most default Linux configurations, there is no "undelete".
- **System Files:** If you accidentally `rm` critical system files, you could render your entire operating system unusable.
- **Typos:** A single misplaced character (`rm myproject` vs. `rm -rf myproject`) could be disastrous.

The `-v` Option: Your Audit Trail

- **`-v` (verbose):** `rm` prints the name of each file as it's deleted. This lets you confirm exactly what has been affected.

Example:

`rm -iv backup_files.zip` (Combines safety of interactive mode with a log of what's gone).

Practice Makes Safer

1. **Dedicated Test Area:** Create a directory called 'test_delete' and some files inside it. Use this for experimentation!
2. **Start Safe:** Practice with `rm -i` to get comfortable with the confirmation process.
3. **Simulate Mistakes:** Deliberately mistype a filename with `rm -i` and see how it protects you.

What About Directories?

By default, `rm` won't delete directories. For that, there's a separate command `rmdir` (which we covered previously), or `rm` with specific options for directory removal.

A Note on Permissions

Sometimes, `rm` will refuse to delete a file even with the right options. This is likely due to **file permissions**. We'll tackle this in a later chapter; there are ways to override permissions if you own the file.

Additional Resources:

- **The `rm` man page (`man rm`):**
  https://www.gnu.org/software/coreutils/manual/html_node/rm-invocation.html
- **Linux File Removal on ExplainShell.com:** https://explainshell.com/

Up Next: Part 2

In the next part of this series, we'll go deeper:

- Exploring the `-r` (recursive) option for deleting entire directory trees.
- Combining `rm` with other commands like `find` to target files based on complex criteria (age, size, etc.).
- Thinking strategically about backups and safety measures in a world where `rm -rf` exists!

Removing Files Unleashed: Commanding the rm for Total File Annihilation, Part 2

In "Removing Files Unleashed: Commanding the rm for Total File Annihilation, Part 2," we go deeper into the powerful and potentially dangerous territory of the rm command. Let's master deletion of entire directories, explore ways of targeting specific files, and discuss safety measures to prevent disasters.

The -r Option: Recursively Deleting Directories

Recall that `rmdir` removes empty directories. For anything containing files or sub-directories, we need rm with the -r (recursive) option.

Scenario: Removing Your Project

```
rm -rf project_folder
```

- **Warning:** This deletes 'project_folder', all its files, any directories within it, the files within *those*, and so on – irreversibly!

rm Power Combos:

We can combine options to great effect:

- **rm -rfv old_backups** Recursively deletes the 'old_backups' directory, prints each file/directory as it's removed, and doesn't ask for confirmation (due to -f).

Selective Targeting with the find Command

Sometimes you need to delete files matching specific criteria. The find command is incredibly powerful, and its output can be fed into rm.

Scenario 1: Old Log Files

```
find /var/log -name '*.log' -mtime +30 -exec rm {} \;
```

Let's dissect this:

- `/var/log`: Where to search
- `-name '*.log'`: Find files ending in '.log'
- `-mtime +30`: Files older than 30 days
- `-exec rm {} \;`: Execute the `rm` command on each file found

Scenario 2: Large Files

`find ~/Downloads -size +50M -exec rm -i {} \;` (Finds files in your Downloads folder over 50MB in size and prompts for deletion confirmation)

Caution: Always Test `find` First

Before the `-exec rm ...` part, run your `find` command alone to *verify* it's selecting the correct files. An error could be disastrous when combined with deletion!

`-r` and Wildcards: Extra Vigilance

Combining recursive deletion with wildcards makes `rm` incredibly potent.

Example (Potentially Dangerous!) `rm -rf /home/my_username/tmp*` (This would wipe out any directory within your home directory starting with "tmp").

Safety Strategies

Let's develop some habits to keep `rm` from wreaking havoc:

1. **The Power of `ls`:** Before deleting, use `ls` with the same patterns to see *exactly* which files would be affected.
2. **Start with `-i`:** The interactive mode is a great safety net while learning.
3. **Backups!:** A robust backup system provides recovery if 'rm' misfires.

A Note on Trash/Recycle Bin

Many Linux desktop environments implement a graphical "Trash". Importantly, command-line `rm` by default usually bypasses this!

Alternatives to `rm`

Some tools offer a middle ground between `rm`'s finality and the graphical Trash:

- **`trash-cli`:** A command-line utility that sends files to a special directory acting as a trash can.
  https://github.com/andreafrancia/trash-cli
- **File Managers with Trash:** Some file managers (like Dolphin or Nautilus) may have trash-can functionality even from the command line.

Additional Resources

- **Explaining `find` with examples:** https://explainshell.com/
- **Safe File Deletion Practices:** https://www.linuxjournal.com/article/1178

Up Next: Part 3

In the final part of this `rm` series, we'll cover:

- The extreme power of combining `rm -rf` with `/` (which targets the root of your file system) and how to prevent catastrophic accidents!
- Advanced recovery options (if they exist) for cases when `rm` removes something you didn't intend.
- Philosophical discussions about balancing the command line's power with responsibility.

Practice Tasks

1. Use the `find` command (without `rm` at first) to locate all files in your home directory that haven't been modified in over a year.
2. Investigate if your Linux system has a command-line utility that implements a "trash" functionality.

Removing Files Unleashed: Commanding the rm for Total File Annihilation, Part 3

Welcome to the final chapter in our "Removing Files Unleashed" series with "Commanding the rm for Total File Annihilation, Part 3." Today, we face the ultimate risk, explore the limits of recovery, and discuss the responsibility that comes with wielding a command as powerful as `rm`.

Understanding the "/" Disaster

Let's talk about the most dangerous scenario: `rm -rf /`

- `/`: This refers to the root of your entire Linux file system.
- `-r`: Recursively deletes everything within the target directory *and* the directory itself.
- `-f`: Forces deletion without asking.

This command, if executed with sufficient permissions, has the potential to obliterate your entire operating system installation! It's the file-system equivalent of a nuclear option.

Prevention is the ONLY Cure

1. **Caution is Paramount:** Think three times, type once. Double-check your paths, wildcards, and `rm` options before hitting Enter.
2. **Non-Root Account:** Where possible, use a day-to-day user account that *lacks* the permissions to wreak havoc at the root level.
3. **"Saftey Net" Aliases:** (Advanced) It's possible to create an alias for `rm` that always defaults to `rm -i`, requiring confirmation.

Recovery After the Fact (It's Not Easy)

- **Immediate Halt:** If you realize you've initiated a disastrous `rm`, stop the process as soon as possible (Ctrl+C in the terminal). You might have saved some data.
- **Undelete Tools:** Some specialized tools *may* be able to recover deleted files from certain file systems if you act quickly. They are not foolproof.

- **Professional Services:** Data recovery companies exist, but their services are expensive and offer no guarantees.
- **The Best Recovery: Backups!** A robust, up-to-date, **offline** backup system is the only way to guarantee you can recover from accidental (or malicious) mass deletions.

File Permissions: A Potential Shield

Remember from previous discussions that each file and directory has permissions controlling who can read, write, or modify it.

- **Root User:** The 'root' user (administrator) usually bypasses most permission checks. rm unleashed by root is supreme.
- **Your User:** Files you own can generally be deleted. If you lack write permission on a directory, you can't delete files inside it, even if you own the files themselves. This offers *some* accidental protection

Responsibility & The Power of the Command Line

Linux trusts you. rm gives you incredible control but assumes you understand the consequences of your actions.

Let's Reflect

- **Alternatives:** Consider graphical file managers. They often have "Trash" concepts, giving you a chance to undo mistakes.
- **Sandboxes:** Practice dangerous commands in a virtual machine or isolated test environment where the worst-case is limited.
- "What If?": Before complex deletions, ask yourself, "What's the worst that could happen if I mistype something?"

Additional Resources

- **Linux File Permissions Deep Dive:** https://linuxjourney.com/lesson/file-permissions
- **Data Recovery Discussion (AskUbuntu):** https://askubuntu.com/ (Search for "undelete files")

Up Next...

Our command-line journey isn't about destruction! Next, we shift gears with:

- The cp command: Safe and controlled copying of files and directories

- The mv command: Moving and renaming, the building blocks of reorganization

Final Thoughts

Treat rm -rf like fire – immensely potent, useful in the right circumstances, but demands respect and caution.

Duplicating Data Realms: Unlocking the cp Command for File Replication, Part 1

Let's dive into the art of copying files in Linux, mastering the cp command's options and the scenarios where it shines.

The Basics of cp

At its core, cp is used to create a duplicate of a file:

- **cp source_file target_file** Creates a copy named 'target_file'. If 'target_file' exists, it is OVERWRITTEN!

Key Points

- **File Content:** cp duplicates the *contents* of the file, not just the filename.
- **Permissions & Timestamps:** By default, the copy may have slightly different permissions and timestamps than the original. We'll learn how to preserve those later.

Scenario 1: Safety Backup

You're working on 'critical_report.odt'. Let's make a backup:

```
cp critical_report.odt critical_report_backup.odt
```

Scenario 2: Distributing a File

You have a setup script. Let's copy it into several user directories:

```
cp install_script.sh /home/john/
cp install_script.sh /home/sarah/
cp install_script.sh /home/ben/
```

Copying Directories: The -r Option

To copy an entire directory along with its contents, we need the -r (recursive) option:

- **cp -r project_files project_backup** Creates a directory 'project_backup' containing a full copy of the 'project_files' structure.

Caution

- Without `-r`, cp will attempt to copy a directory as if it were a regular file, likely resulting in errors.
- An existing 'project_backup' would be overwritten, so use unique target names!

Essential Options for Control

Let's enhance our cp mastery:

- **`-i` (Interactive):** Just like `rm`, prompts for confirmation before overwriting an existing file.
- **`-v` (Verbose):** Prints what's being copied, providing feedback.
- **`-u` (Update):** Only copies the source file if it's newer than the target, or the target doesn't exist. Great for syncing changes.
- **`-p` (Preserve):** Attempts to copy as much metadata as possible - timestamps, ownership, permissions.

Scenario 3: Careful Updates

Let's update our backup, but only if the original file has changed:

```
cp -uv critical_report.odt critical_report_backup.odt
```

Practice

1. You have a directory 'website_templates' with the structure of your website. Create a full backup named 'website_backup_2023_11_18'.
2. You modify some files in 'website_templates'. Practice using cp with appropriate options to update only the changed files within your backup folder.

File Preservation vs. Quick Updates

- Need an exact, timestamp-matching backup? Use `cp -rp`.
- Need to quickly sync changes to another location? Use `cp -uv`.

What About Wildcards?

It's tempting to use wildcards like `cp *.jpg new_folder` to copy multiple files. **Proceed with caution!** If 'new_folder' doesn't exist, you might end up with all your JPGs lumped together with the same name, overwriting each other.

Additional Resources

- **man cp:** The definitive manual page for the cp command. https://www.gnu.org/software/coreutils/manual/html_node/cp-invocation.html
- **Copying Files and Directories on ExplainShell:** https://explainshell.com/

Up Next: Part 2

In the next part, we'll cover:

- Copying between different storage devices and remote systems.
- Advanced techniques for selectively copying files based on patterns.
- Strategies for large-scale copying operations.

Duplicating Data Realms: Unlocking the cp Command for File Replication, Part 2

In "Duplicating Data Realms: Unlocking the cp Command for File Replication, Part 2," we go beyond basic copies and explore scenarios where cp proves its versatility across devices, remote systems, and complex synchronization tasks.

Crossing Boundaries: Copying Between Devices

Often you'll need to copy files to or from USB drives, external disks, or network shares. Linux represents these as mounted directories within the file system.

Prerequisites

1. **The Device: Is it connected and recognized?** Some tools like lsblk can help you list block devices, but graphical file managers often provide user-friendly device names.
2. **Mount Point: Where is it?** USB drives might appear under /media/your_username/ or /mnt.

Scenario: Archiving to USB

Let's assume your drive is mounted at /media/your_username/backup_drive

```
cp -r project_files
/media/your_username/backup_drive/project_backup
```

Copying Over Networks with scp

The scp (secure copy) command is built on the SSH protocol, enabling file transfers to and from remote Linux systems.

Syntax:

```
scp source_file username@remote_host:/path/on/remote
```

Scenario: Website Backup to a Remote Server

```
scp -r website_templates
adminuser@backup_server.com:/home/adminuser/backups
```

Important

- **SSH:** The remote system must have an SSH server running.
- **Permissions:** Your user needs permissions to write to the target location on the remote machine.

Selective Copies

Let's get more sophisticated by using patterns and file attributes for our copies.

Scenario 1: Images from Multiple Sources

You have photos scattered in different folders. Consolidate them:

```
cp /home/username/holiday_photos/*.jpg
/home/username/pictures/organized
cp /home/username/documents/2022_pics/*.png
/home/username/pictures/organized
```

Scenario 2: Modified in the Last Week

Use the `find` command from our 'rm' chapters to target files, then copy:

```
find /path/to/work -type f -mtime -7 -exec cp {}
/path/to/backup \;
```

Synchronization with `rsync`

The `rsync` command is the king of efficient file mirroring and syncing. Features include:

- **Delta Transfers:** Copies only the changed portions of files. Great for large backups over slow links.
- **Deletion Synchronization:** (`--delete` option) Can make the target an exact mirror, removing files not present in the source.
- **Compression:** Built-in compression to reduce network traffic.

Scenario: Offsite Website Mirroring

```
rsync -avz /var/www/website_files
adminuser@backup_server.com:/backups/website
```
(a: archive mode, v: verbose, z: compression)

Additional Resources

- **Linux `mount` command Explained:**
  https://linuxize.com/post/how-to-use-the-mount-command-in-linux/
- **`scp` examples:**
  https://linuxize.com/post/how-to-use-scp-command-to-securely-transfer-files/
- **`rsync` Power User Guide:** https://linux.die.net/man/1/rsync

Beyond Copying: The World of Data Management

While `cp` is a foundation, let's think strategically:

- **Versioning:** For critical projects, use version control systems (like Git) for more structured history tracking than simple copies provide.
- **Large-Scale Data:** Tools specifically designed for vast dataset management may be more efficient than raw `cp`.
- **Scheduling:** `cron` (we'll discuss this later) lets you automate backups and copies on a schedule.

Practice

1. Design a command or short script using `cp` or `rsync` to back up your home directory to an external drive, excluding temporary files and large video files.
2. (Advanced): Research a remote backup service compatible with `rsync`. Set up a test where you synchronize a directory with your remote backup.

Up Next

Coming up, the `mv` command! We'll shift from duplication to relocation and renaming, adding another dimension to file organization mastery.

Shifting and Shaping: Mastering File Movement and Renaming with the mv Command, Part 1

The mv command is a powerhouse of file organization, allowing us to relocate files and change their names. Let's get moving!

Fundamentals of mv

1. Moving a File:

```bash
mv source_file target_directory
```

* Moves 'source_file' into the 'target_directory'.
* If the 'target_directory' doesn't exist, it's treated as a filename (renaming, see below).

2. Renaming a File:

```bash
mv old_filename new_filename
```

* Renames 'old_filename' to 'new_filename' within the *same* directory.

Key Points

- **Overwriting:** mv will overwrite an existing file in the destination if the names match!
- **Directories Too:** mv can also move entire directories, including their contents.

Scenario 1: Organizing Downloads

You have a messy 'Downloads' folder:

```
mv presentation.pdf Documents/
```

```
mv holiday_photos.jpg Pictures/
mv project_backup.zip /tmp/backups
```

Scenario 2: Fixing a Typo

You misspelled a filename, "inut.txt" instead of "input.txt":

```
mv inut.txt input.txt
```

Essential Options

Let's enhance our control over moves and renames:

- **-i (Interactive):** Prompts before overwriting, a safeguard against errors.
- **-v (Verbose):** Explains what mv is doing.
- **-n (No Overwrite):** Prevents overwriting existing files. Useful for testing your commands.
- **-u (Update):** Only moves the file if it's newer than the destination file, or the destination doesn't exist. Avoids unnecessary copying.

Scenario 3: Careful Renaming

You want to change several '.jpg' files to '.jpeg' but avoid accidentally overwriting existing files:

```
mv -vn *.jpg *.jpeg
```

Moving Across Devices

Recall from our cp chapters that mounted USB drives or network shares appear as part of your file system. mv works seamlessly to shift files between these locations just as if they were on the same drive.

Tip: Always Double-Check

Before executing any complex mv command, especially when using wildcards, use ls to visualize what files would be affected. Prevention is better than a cure!

Small Command, Big Possibilities

We've just scratched the surface of mv's capabilities:

- **Bulk Renaming:** Using wildcards or clever scripting, mv can rename groups of files systematically.
- **Implicit Backup:** `mv file.txt file.txt.bak` creates a quick backup before modifying the original.

Additional Resources:

- **The mv man page:** https://www.gnu.org/software/coreutils/manual/html_node/mv-invocation.html
- **Interactive mv Practice:** https://explainshell.com/

Up Next: Part 2

In the next part, we'll combine mv with other commands for streamlined workflows, learn advanced multi-file moves, and explore strategies to use mv without leaving our comfort zone of text editors.

Tasks for Practice

1. Your home directory is littered with '.log' files. Create a directory 'old_logs' and move all the log files into it.
2. You have several files named 'draft_1.txt', 'draft_2.txt' etc. Explore renaming them systematically to 'project_draft_1.txt', 'project_draft_2.txt', and so on. (Hint: There are ways to do this with mv and a little scripting!)

Shifting and Shaping: Mastering File Movement and Renaming with the mv Command, Part 2

In "Shifting and Shaping: Mastering File Movement and Renaming with the mv Command, Part 2," we journey deeper into mv's power, combining it with other commands for streamlined workflows and exploring how to use its file manipulation abilities from the comfort of our favorite text editors.

mv + find: Targeted File Operations

Recall our discussion of the find command from the rm chapters. Let's combine it with mv for precise file relocation:

Scenario 1: Gathering MP3s

You have music scattered everywhere:

```
find /home/username -name '*.mp3' -exec mv {}
/home/username/Music \;
```

- find locates all MP3s within your home directory.
- -exec mv {} \; executes the mv command, the '{}' representing each file found, moving them to your Music directory.

Scenario 2: Archiving Old Logs

Find log files older than 30 days and move them:

```
find /var/log -name '*.log' -mtime +30 -exec mv {}
/var/log/archive \;
```

Cautions

- **Test with echo:** Before running a complex find...mv command, replace mv with echo to preview what *would* happen.
- **Permissions:** Make sure you have write permission to the target directory.

Bulk Renaming Power

While mv can handle simple renames, sometimes we need more sophisticated transformations. Here are some approaches:

1. The `rename` Utility

- **Not to be confused with the 'rename' built into some shells**
- Install with your package manager (e.g., `sudo apt install rename` on Debian-based systems)
- Syntax using regular expressions for complex renaming

Example:

`rename 's/\.TXT$/\.txt/' *.TXT` (Changes all uppercase '.TXT' extensions to lowercase)

2. Text Editors as Renaming Tools

- Many text editors have "Find and Replace" features that operate on filenames within a directory:
    - **Nano:** Ctrl+R can batch-rename files you've opened
    - **Graphical Editors:** Often have "Rename" on files in the project view.

3. The Power of the Shell (Advanced)

Using a combination of `ls`, wildcards, text manipulation tools (`sed`, `awk`) and loops within a shell script, you could perform nearly any renaming task imaginable!

Additional Resources

- **rename utility explained:**
  https://linuxize.com/post/rename-files-in-linux/

mv Isn't Always Essential

Many commands have the ability to *create new* files as an output of their operation:

- `cp source modified_copy`: Effectively renaming during a copy.
- **Text Editors:** "Save As" gives you a new filename.

- **Redirection:** `some_command > new_output_file` creates a file named 'new_output_file'.

Strategic Thinking

The best solution might combine `mv` for bulk moves based on existing filenames, and other tools for cases where filenames are generated as part of the process you're doing.

Up Next (Future Chapters)

- **The `file` Command:** Identifying file types, crucial before operations, especially when mixing scripts and `mv`.
- **Handling Spaces and Special Characters:** Filenames aren't always cooperative! We'll learn escaping techniques.
- **Auto-Completion:** Making `mv` even easier

Practice

1. Within a test directory, use a text editor to create files named 'Project_Report_v1.txt', 'Project_Report_v2.txt'... Write a short script using a loop, `mv`, and string manipulation to rename them to the format 'Report_01.txt', 'Report_02.txt' etc. (Hint: String manipulation in Bash can involve `${variable#prefix_to_remove}`)
2. (Advanced): Research more sophisticated usage of the `rename` utility.

Unveiling File Identities: Decoding File Types with the file Command, Part 1

Get ready to go beyond mere filenames as we learn to peer into the true heart of files with the `file` utility. Understanding file types is vital for ensuring you're using the right commands and to troubleshoot mysterious data.

Why File Type Matters

- **Compatibility:** Using 'image_editor.exe' on a PDF will get you nowhere! The `file` command acts as a safeguard.
- **Behavior:** Linux often determines how to handle a file based on its type, not just the extension.
- **Security:** A file masquerading as something harmless (like 'picture.jpg' that's actually an executable) can be a security risk. `file` helps spot these.

The Basics of file

The `file` command has a refreshingly simple core syntax:

```
file filename1 filename2 ...
```

Scenario 1: Single File

```
file report.docx
```

Output might be: `report.docx: Microsoft Word 2007+`

Scenario 2: Many Files

```
file *.mp3
```

Analyzes all MP3s in the current directory.

How Does file Know?

1. **File Extensions:** A first clue, but easily faked.
2. **"Magic Bytes":** Files often have headers or internal patterns specific to their type. `file` has a database of these.
3. **Content Analysis:** Performs deeper tests if needed, like looking for text patterns in documents.

`file` in Action

Let's make things interesting!

1. The Misleading Extension

You have 'picture.txt', but it won't display. Why?

`file picture.txt` Output: `picture.txt: JPEG image data` ...aha! Rename it to 'picture.jpg'

2. The Unknown Download

You downloaded 'important_data' with no extension. What is it?

`file important_data` Output: `important_data: gzip compressed data` (Treat it as a .gz archive)

3. The Corrupted File

Backup software throws an error about 'project_backup'. Is it salvageable?

`file project_backup`

- Output: `project_backup: Zip archive data` (Good! There's likely a way to fix the archive itself)
- Output: `project_backup: data` (Uh oh, deeper damage)

Key Options

- **-b (Brief):** Don't print the filename, just the type. Useful in scripts.
- **-i (MIME Type):** Outputs the file's MIME type (e.g., 'image/jpeg') important for web-related work.

Limitations of `file`

- **Not Foolproof:** Clever disguises can sometimes fool it.
- **Database Dependent:** If `file`'s database doesn't recognize a rare format, it might fail.
- **Not an *Analysis* Tool:** Tells you the format, not if the file contents themselves are valid. You'd need specialized tools for that.

Additional Resources

- `man file` https://man7.org/linux/man-pages/man1/file.1.html

Up Next: Part 2

In the next part, we'll:

- **Integrate `file` with other commands:** Find all text files, identify PNG images specifically, and more.
- **Explore filesystems where extensions are less common.**
- **Troubleshooting scenarios based on real-world examples.**

Practice

1. Create a text file, but give it a '.pdf' extension. Can you 'trick' the `file` command?
2. Find a few image files (JPEG, PNG, GIF etc.) Is there any difference in how `file` describes them?

Unveiling File Identities: Decoding File Types with the file Command, Part 2

In "Unveiling File Identities: Decoding File Types with the file Command, Part 2," we'll dive deeper into scenarios where `file` becomes our command-line detective, and learn to combine its insights with the power of other tools.

Using `file` with Other Commands

1. **Filtering with `find`**

    Locate all MP3s *specifically* for cleanup:

    ```
    find . -type f -name '*.mp3' -exec file {} \; | grep
    'MPEG ADTS'
    ```

(Note: The 'MPEG ADTS…' will filter the output to show true MP3s as per `file`'s identification).

2. **Conditional Operations**

    Let's say we only want to move JPEG images, not other file types:

    ```
    for f in *.jpg; do
      if file "$f" | grep -q 'JPEG image data'; then
        mv "$f" /path/to/images
      fi
    done
    ```

`file` in Different Environments

- **Non-Standard File Extensions:** Many other operating systems don't rely on extensions as heavily. `file` is crucial here.
- **Network Shares:** When accessing files remotely, extensions might not be reliable.
- **Embedded Systems:** Devices with limited Linux installations often still include `file` to analyze unknown data.

Practice Scenario: Fixing a Website (Slightly Advanced)

You inherit a broken website. Images don't load. Here's our detective work:

1. **Existence:** Does `uploads/cute_cat.jpg` actually exist? (Use `ls` to check)
2. **Permissions:** Can the web server *read *the file? (Chapter on permissions coming later)
3. **The Imposter:**

   ```
   file uploads/cute_cat.jpg
   ```

Output: `uploads/cute_cat.jpg: HTML document text`...Aha! Wrong file type entirely.

Troubleshooting: When `file` Output Is Ambiguous

- **"ASCII Text":** Too generic! Use text editors (`nano`, `less`) to look inside the file for hints of its true structure.
- **"Data":** Extremely vague. There might be partial corruption, or the format is too obscure for `file`. Specialized format identification tools would be needed (often web-based).

Beyond Simple Identification

Some files contain rich metadata that file can extract:

Scenario: Photo Metadata

```
file summer_trip.jpg
```

Output might include:

- Image Dimensions
- Camera Model
- Date Taken (if the camera stored it)
- Even GPS coordinates!

Advanced: Scripting with Metadata

You could write scripts to sort photos by date taken, find photos from a specific camera model, etc., using this extracted metadata.

Additional Resources

- **Metadata Extractors:** Specialized tools exist for audio, particular image formats, etc. Search based on the file type you need.

Up Next (Future Chapters)

- **Handling Filenames with Spaces and Special Characters:** How to work with files when the filenames themselves are tricky to type.
- **Command-Line Shortcuts:** Time-saving key combinations for faster navigation and file operations.

File-Type Puzzles

Have you had a stubborn file where `file`'s analysis was a key part of solving the problem?

Let's Learn Together

Are there any specific types of files you regularly work with, where knowing the precise internal format is important (e.g., scientific data, financial documents)? How do you currently identify these?

Taming Spaces in the Wild: Navigating Filenames with Spaces, Part 1

File systems treat spaces as separators, so filenames like "Project Report.docx" and "vacation photos" can turn from convenient to disastrous in the command line if we're not careful.

Why Spaces Wreak Havoc

Let's illustrate the problem:

1. **Naive ls:**

   ```
   ls vacation photos
   ```

   Linux thinks you want to list files named 'vacation' *and* a separate file named 'photos'. Errors ensue!

2. **rm Mischief:**

   ```
   rm project report.docx
   ```

   Potentially deletes files named 'project' and 'report.docx', likely NOT your intention.

The Core Concept: Quoting

In the command line, we use quotes to tell the shell "treat this whole thing as one unit, even if it has spaces inside."

- **Double Quotes (" ")** Allow some interpretation within (we'll get to that in Part 2)
- **Single Quotes (' ')** Very literal, everything inside is treated as plain text.

Scenario 1: Touching a File with Spaces

```
touch "My Vacation Report.txt"
```

Creates a *single* file with the intended name.

Scenario 2: Safely Removing

```
rm "Project Report.docx"
```

Now, only the file with the spaces in its name is deleted.

Methods of Quoting

1. **Enclosing the Whole Filename:** As seen above, `"Filename With Spaces.ext"`
2. **Escape Characters:** The backslash (\) placed *directly* before a space. Example: `my\ vacation\ photos` is treated as "my vacation photos".

When to Choose Which

- **Simple Spaces:** Either quoting or the backslash escape works fine.
- **Special Characters:** (Part 2!) Things like '$', or '*' need more careful quoting, as the shell interprets these separately.

Caveats: Graphical Tools vs. Terminal

- File managers often visually show a single file even if it has spaces, and let you rename, etc. They're hiding the quoting from you!
- Some commands have built-in ways to handle spaces without you needing to quote.

Practice Makes Perfect

Create a 'test' directory and deliberately make files and subdirectories with spaces in their names. Then practice the following:

- **`ls`-ing Them:** Do it with and without quotes to see the difference.
- **`cd`-ing Into Them:** Get comfortable navigating into these directories.
- **Copying with `cp` and Moving with `mv`:** Ensure you preserve the spaces.

Extra: Quoting Within Scripts

If you write shell scripts (`bash`, etc.) the rules of quoting become even more important, as now it's the script interpreting things, not just your interactive session.

Additional Resources

- **Quoting explanation on ExplainShell:** https://explainshell.com/ (Include examples with spaces)
- **Safe File Deletion Practices:** https://www.linuxjournal.com/article/1178

Up Next: Part 2

- Handling spaces *and* other unusual characters like '$', '(', etc.
- When double quotes behave differently than single quotes.
- The power of auto-completion to minimize our need to type spaces directly!

Taming Spaces in the Wild: Navigating Filenames with Spaces, Part 2

Now that we've mastered the basics of quoting and escaping spaces, let's face scenarios where filenames include *both* spaces and other trickster characters that the shell loves to interpret.

When Spaces Aren't Enough: Other Special Characters

Characters like these have specific meanings in the command line:

- **Dollar Sign ($)**: Variables (we'll cover these later)
- **Asterisk (*)**: Wildcards for matching patterns
- **Exclamation Point (!)**: Command history
- **Parenthesis, Brackets, Ampersand, etc.** Each has potential special uses

Scenario 1: The "$10 Discount.txt" Problem

Let's say you want to view this text file:

```
cat $10 Discount.txt
```

Whoops! The shell might try to interpret '$10' as a variable name. Solution? Quoting!

- `" $10 Discount.txt"` works in most cases.

Scenario 2: Wildcards Gone Wild

You have several files: `Project(final).doc`, `Project(v2).doc`

`rm Project*.doc` might intend to delete old versions, but the * will be expanded, potentially catching and deleting your precious `Project(final).doc` as well!

- `"Project*.doc"` is usually safer

Nesting Quotes

Sometimes you need to use single quotes *inside* double quotes. Why?

- **Variables Inside Quoted Text:**

```
echo "Today's date is: $(date)"
```

The `$(date)` part is executed *within* the overall quoted string

- **Precise Control:** Single quotes within double quotes are treated literally even if they contain characters like $.

Best Practices

1. **Avoid the Problem:** Name files thoughtfully! Underscores (_) or hyphens (-) instead of spaces make life easier.
2. **Quote When Unsure:** If a filename *might* cause issues, a quick quote is safer than troubleshooting errors afterwards.
3. **Autocomplete Is Your Friend!** (Next chapter) Tab completion in the terminal often fills in filenames *and* adds necessary quoting for you.

When Things Get Complex (Beyond Basics)

- **Regular Expressions:** For sophisticated pattern matching in commands (grep, find, etc.) there's a whole world of special characters and quoting rules.
- **Script Writing:** In shell scripts, the quoting game becomes an art form for reliability.

Additional Resources

- **Linux quoting cheat sheet:** https://mywiki.wooledge.org/Quotes
- **Regular Expressions tutorials:** https://regexone.com/

Practical Challenge

1. **Create a "Messy Names" Directory:** Fill it with files with spaces, dollar signs, brackets, etc.
2. **Practice:** Use ls, cd, mv, cp, and text viewing commands (cat, less) to successfully work within that directory without causing errors.

Embracing Special Characters: Conquering Filename Challenges, Part 1

We've tackled spaces; now let's face the whole range of characters that can make filenames either delightfully descriptive or a command-line nightmare.

Why Special Characters Can Be Tricky

Many characters beyond spaces have specific meanings to the Linux shell (the program interpreting your commands):

- **Wildcards:**
    - `*` (matches zero or more characters)
    - `?` (matches any single character)
- **Redirection:**
    - `>` (send command output to a file)
    - `<` (take a file as command input)
- **Pipes:** `|` (connect the output of one command to the input of another)
- **Logical Operators:**
    - `&&` (run a command only if the previous succeeded)
    - `||` (run a command only if the previous failed)
- **Background Jobs:** `&` (run a command in the background)

…and many more!

Scenario 1: The Peril of the Parenthesis

You have files named 'Project Notes (1).txt' and 'Project Notes (2).txt'. Let's try to delete the first one:

```
rm Project Notes (1).txt
```

Oops! The shell might try to interpret the parenthesis, leading to errors or unexpected results.

Scenario 2: Wildcards Gone Rogue

You want to list files like 'Report_v1.pdf', 'Report_v2.pdf', etc.

```
ls Report_*.pdf
```

If you have a file named 'Report_notes.pdf' it would get included as well!

The Core Techniques

Familiar tactics with a twist for special characters:

1. **Quoting (Double Quotes Preferred):** `"Project Notes (1).txt"` Usually preserves the special meaning of most characters within the quotes, allowing safe execution of commands.
2. **Escaping with Backslash ():** Placing " directly before the special character tells the shell to ignore its special meaning this one time.
3. **Single Quotes (For Extreme Literalness):** Nearly everything within single quotes is treated as plain text by the shell.

When Double Quotes Aren't Enough

- **$ (Variables):** Inside double quotes, the shell *will* try to expand variables. Single quotes or escaping with " prevents this.
- **Nesting:** Sometimes you need combinations of quoting and escaping for complex filenames.

Example: Money Troubles

File named "$50 budget.txt". Let's `cat` it:

- **Fails:** `cat $50 budget.txt` (Looks for a variable named '50')
- **Works 1:** `cat "$50 budget.txt"`
- **Works 2:** `cat \$50 budget.txt`

Best Practices

- **Prevention:** When naming files, stick to letters, numbers, underscores (_), hyphens (-) and periods (.) for the simplest command-line life.
- **Know Your Needs:** If filenames MUST contain special characters, master quoting and escaping.
- **Autocomplete for the Win!** (Upcoming Chapter) Tab completion can save a ton of hassle.

Additional Resources

- **Shell Special Characters List:** https://tldp.org/LDP/abs/html/special-chars.html

- **Quoting in Shell Scripts:**
  https://www.gnu.org/software/bash/manual/html_node/Quoting.html
  (Gets complex!)

Up Next: Part 2

- **More complex scenarios mixing spaces AND special characters**
- **How Autocomplete makes special characters less scary**
- **File Renaming Tools to help 'fix' bad filenames**

Practice Challenge

Create files with names like:

- `Report & Statistics.xlsx`
- `Vacation Photos (Best!).jpg`
- `$100 Invoice.pdf`

Now practice:

- Using `ls` safely to list them.
- Deleting them with `rm`
- Viewing their contents with text-based commands (`cat`, `less`)

Embracing Special Characters: Conquering Filename Challenges, Part 2

In "Embracing Special Characters: Conquering Filename Challenges, Part 2," we'll face the ultimate trials: when tricky filenames combine spaces, dollar signs, brackets, and everything in between! Plus, we'll see how to leverage tools to fight back against chaotic naming.

When Chaos Descends: Spaces + Special Characters

Scenario 1: Calculations Gone Wrong

```
Budget ($10 Savings).ods
```

Try to calculate: `echo $(( $(cat Budget\ ($10\ Savings).ods ) + 50 ))`

This likely breaks! Double quotes, single quotes, escaping…it gets messy fast.

Scenario 2: Wildcards + Parenthesis

```
Project Notes (draft 1).txt … Project Notes (draft 2).txt
… etc.
```

You want to delete only `(draft 1)`. Wildcards become dangerous!

Key Strategies

1. **Prioritize Escaping:** If you can get away with escaping individual special characters, this is often the simplest approach.
2. **Fall Back to Single Quotes:** When escaping gets too complex, single quotes often treat the entire filename literally.
3. **Embrace Complexity (When Needed):** Nesting different types of quotes for fine-grained control.

Example: Fixing the Calculation

- **Escaping:** `cat Budget\ (\$10\ Savings\).ods` (might work, but depends on context)
- **Single Quotes:** `cat 'Budget ($10 Savings).ods'` (usually safer)

Autocomplete: Our Mighty Ally (More in the next chapter!)

Most shells have tab-based autocomplete. When you start typing a filename and press Tab:

- It automatically fills in as much of the tricky filename as possible.
- Often adds necessary quotes or escapes *for you!*

When Prevention Fails: Renaming Tools

Sometimes, the best solution is to fix the filenames themselves.

1. **Graphical File Managers:** Most let you rename with special characters easily.
2. **Command-Line Renaming Tools:**
   - `rename` (preinstalled on some systems) - Uses pattern-based renaming
   - More specific tools exist for file types like music, photos, etc.

Example: Sanitizing with `rename` (Syntax can be tricky, so research first!)

```
rename 's/\s+/_/g' *      # Replaces all spaces with underscores
rename 's/[()]//g'  *     # Removes parentheses globally
```

Important Notes

- **Always Back Up:** Before mass renaming, backup important files!
- **Test First:** Use rename options to preview changes before applying them.

Additional Resources

- **rename command:** https://linux.die.net/man/1/rename
- **File renaming tools:** Search based on your specific needs (photo renaming, etc.)

Up Next: The Tab Trick

We'll learn how autocomplete makes special characters AND navigating directories less intimidating, allowing us to often avoid typing the complexities directly.

Practice

On top of your previous 'messy files' practice:

- **cd: Change directory** into a directory containing files with various special characters.
- **mv + cp:** Rename and copy those files while preserving the tricky names.
- **Text Manipulation:** Use commands like grep or head on them.

The Tab Trick Unveiled: Harnessing Auto-Completion for Command and File Mastery, Part 1

Get ready to streamline your command-line life! Autocomplete isn't just about laziness; it's about accuracy, speed, and even discovering new abilities within Linux.

What is Auto-Completion (and Why You Should Care)

1. **Typing Less:** Press the Tab key, and the shell tries to complete what you've started typing (command, filename, etc.).
2. **Error Reduction:** Misspelling a long filename? Autocomplete helps! Plus, it exposes those tricky special characters, so you're less likely to make mistakes with them.
3. **Exploration:** Don't know the exact command? Tab can suggest some! Ever forget which subdirectories exist? Tab to the rescue.

How It Works (The Basics)

- **Possible Matches:** The shell looks at available commands, filenames in the current directory, and sometimes even other options depending on the context.
- **Single Match:** If only one thing matches what you've typed so far, it auto-completes it!
- **Multiple Matches:**
    - Partial completion as far as it can.
    - A second Tab press often lists the possible options.

Scenario 1: Tedious Typing

You're in a directory with 'Very_Long_And_Descriptive_Report.pdf'.

Without autocomplete: `less Very_Long_And_Descriptive_Report.pdf`

With autocomplete:

1. Type `less V` and hit Tab
2. It likely completes the whole filename for you!

Scenario 2: "What Was That Command Again?"

You did something with image files a while back. Commands starting with 'im…' ?

1. Type `im` and press Tab twice. You might get a list like: `imagemagick import`

Autocomplete + Special Characters

Autocomplete becomes a lifesaver when dealing with those filenames containing spaces, brackets, and everything in between:

1. **Start Typing:** Type the beginning of the tricky filename.
2. **Hit Tab:** The shell often automatically adds quotes or escapes, making the whole thing usable in your command.

Important Notes

- **Context is Key:** Autocomplete is smartest with commands at the *beginning* of a line, and filenames when placed after a command.
- **Case Sensitivity:** Linux cares about uppercase/lowercase
- **Customizations:** Advanced shells have even fancier autocomplete features you can configure.

Additional Resources

- **Shell Specifics:** Search for things like "bash autocomplete" for your Linux distribution to discover more features.

Up Next: Part 2

- **Autocomplete for Directory Navigation (it's not just filenames!)**
- **Power-User tricks to make autocomplete even faster**
- **Troubleshooting when it doesn't behave as expected**

Practice

1. **Intentionally Misspell:** Type the start of a command or filename incorrectly, then try Tab. See how it helps you spot the error.
2. **The Exploration Game:** Go into a directory with various files. Type a single letter, then hit Tab twice. Repeat with different letters. See what the shell suggests.

Pro Tip

If autocomplete isn't working as expected:

- Make sure you're typing at the start of a command, or directly after one.
- Check if your Linux distribution needs specific setup to enable fancier autocomplete

Share Your Victories

Has autocomplete ever saved you from a complex command-line headache?

The Tab Trick Unveiled: Harnessing Auto-Completion for Command and File Mastery, Part 2

In "The Tab Trick Unveiled, Part 2," let's venture further into the realm of autocomplete mastery, making complex directory navigation a breeze, and supercharging your command-line efficiency.

Autocomplete for Navigating Directories

1. **The Power of Partial Paths:** Start typing a directory name, hit Tab!
   - Example: cd Docu *[Tab]* might complete to cd Documents/
2. **Deeper Journeys:** Keep typing and Tab-completing. cd Documents/Pers *[Tab]* could complete to cd Documents/Personal/
3. **Subdirectories Revealed:** Stuck mid-path? Try Tab twice to see what's inside the current part-way typed directory.

Scenario: Buried Treasure

You have a Project Files/2023/March/Report_v2.pdf file somewhere.

- cd Pr *[Tab*] might autocomplete to 'Project Files/'
- Keep going: cd Project\ Files/20 *[Tab]*
- ... and so on, until you reach your destination.

Efficiency Boost

- **Less Typing = Fewer Mistakes:** Particularly with long, nested paths.
- **Discoverability:** Forgot the exact subdirectory name? Autocomplete can jog your memory.

Autocomplete Superpowers (May Vary)

Certain advanced shells offer:

- **Mid-Command Completion:** In commands like less Documents/P *[Tab]* it might fill in the rest of the filename.

- **Inline Suggestions:** Instead of completing, they *ghost* possible completions next to your cursor.

Practice: The Maze

1. Create a directory structure with a few levels of nesting. Place some files inside.
2. **Close Your Eyes!** (Figuratively). Try navigating *only* using autocomplete, from the top directory down to a specific file.
3. **Extra:** Try the cp or mv commands, letting autocomplete help with both the source and destination paths.

Troubleshooting Autocomplete

- **Nothing Happens:** Ensure basic autocomplete is enabled for your shell. (Distribution-specific, so search online).
- **Completes Unexpectedly:** You might be mid-word within a command. Autocomplete is often context-sensitive.
- **Incorrect Completion:** The shell is guessing the best it can. More specific typing on your part usually fixes it.

Customization

Advanced shells let you tweak autocomplete behavior:

- **Strictness:** Complete only if there's an exact match, or allow for partial?
- **Visuals:** How suggestions are displayed while you type.

Additional Resources

- **Autocomplete in Different Shells:** Search "[your shell name] autocomplete" for customizations and power-user tips.

Up Next (Future Chapters)

- **Essential Keyboard Shortcuts (Beyond Just Tab!):** Make navigating and editing commands even smoother.
- **Command-Line History:** Autocomplete lets you re-use parts of past commands as well!

Expert Tips

- **Combine with Wildcards:** If you know the start of a filename and its general location, a wildcard + Tab can be a potent combo.

- **Speed Matters:** Autocomplete shines when you build muscle memory. Consistent practice is key!

Your 'Aha!' Autocomplete Moments

Has autocomplete ever gotten you out of a tight spot where you were unsure of an exact filename or path?

Command Line Conveniences: Unlocking Essential Keyboard Shortcuts, Part 1

Get ready to level up your command-line speed and agility with "Command Line Conveniences: Unlocking Essential Keyboard Shortcuts, Part 1." Think less typing, more efficiency, and seriously smooth navigation!

Why Shortcuts Matter

- **Speed Boost:** Frequent actions become lightning-fast. Imagine hopping around directories or editing commands without constantly reaching for the mouse.
- **Reduced Errors:** Fewer keystrokes means fewer chances for typos. This is especially important when dealing with file operations where mistakes can have consequences.
- **Workflow Zen:** Once muscle memory kicks in, using the command line becomes a fluid, almost instinctive experience.

Core Concepts

- **The Ctrl Key (Control):** Combo time! Many shortcuts involve holding Ctrl and pressing another key.
- **The Alt Key (Alternate):** Used for alternative functions in certain commands and text editors.
- **Arrow Keys:** These familiar friends are even mightier on the command line.

Scenario 1: Tedious Retyping

You type `cd Documents/2023_Project/Reports`. Oops, a typo! Without shortcuts, you might retype the *entire* command.

Scenario 2: Lost in History

You need a command from earlier. Without shortcuts, it's scrolling or retyping time.

The Essential Shortcuts – Part 1

1. Movement Within a Line

- **Ctrl+A:** Jump to the beginning of the line.
- **Ctrl+E:** Jump to the end of the line.
- **Left/Right Arrows:** Move one character at a time (you knew this one, but it's vital!).

2. Editing on the Fly

- **Ctrl+U:** Delete everything *before* your cursor on the current line.
- **Ctrl+K:** Delete everything *after* your cursor.
- **Ctrl+W:** Delete the word before your cursor.

3. Recalling Past Commands

- **Up/Down Arrows:** Cycle through your command history. Hit Enter to execute a command from your history.

Making It Stick: Practical Exercises

1. **The Retyping Challenge:** Type a moderately long command path with a deliberate mistake in the middle. Now, use movement and editing shortcuts to fix it *without* retyping the whole thing.
2. **History Hunt:**
   - Type a few different commands.
   - Now, use *only* the Up arrow to step back through them, re-running them with Enter.
3. **Mix and Match:** Start with a long command. Now:
   - Use Ctrl+A and Ctrl+E to jump to the start/end.
   - Delete a portion with Ctrl+U or Ctrl+K
   - Use arrows and Ctrl+W to make some word-level edits.

Additional Notes

- **Shells Matter:** Some shells have *even more* shortcuts, or let you customize them.
- **Applications Within the Terminal:** Text editors like Nano (future chapter) have their own shortcut sets.

Additional Resources

- **Bash Shortcuts Cheat Sheet:**
  https://linuxize.com/post/bash-keyboard-shortcuts/

Up Next: Part 2

- **More advanced command editing (transposing letters, etc.)**
- **Maximizing command-line recall with history tricks**
- **Taming text file editing (if it fits within file operations)**

Pro Tip

Start by mastering a few shortcuts at a time. Integrate them into your daily command-line habits, and gradually add more.

Share Your Shortcut Discoveries

Do you have a favorite, perhaps lesser-known, shortcut that has saved you time and headaches?

Command Line Conveniences: Unlocking Essential Keyboard Shortcuts, Part 2

Get ready to power up your command-line workflow with shortcuts focused on editing, history, and overall efficiency.

Mastering Command Editing

1. Jumping Between Words

- **Ctrl + Left/Right Arrows:** Hop to the beginning/end of the previous/next word. Great for fixing a typo within a word, without affecting the rest of your command.

2. Transposing Characters

- **Alt+T:** Swaps the character *before* your cursor with the one *under* your cursor. Amazingly useful for those pesky, one-letter typos.

3. Yank and Paste (Some Shells)

- **Ctrl+Y:** "Yank" (copy) previously deleted text (deleted with Ctrl+K, etc.)
- **Ctrl+P:** "Paste" what you yanked.

Note: These yank/paste features may not work in all terminals, but are super handy when available.

Harnessing Command History

1. **Beyond Up/Down Arrow:** The basics are great, but there's more…
2. **Search History:**
   - **Ctrl+R:** Start typing, and it searches backwards through your command history for matches. Hit Ctrl+R again to cycle matches if there's more than one.
3. **Execute Without Searching:**
   - **!prefix:** Run the most recent command starting with "prefix". Example: !ls would re-run your last ls command.

Scenario: The Long Command Fix

You ran a complex command with a few options: `find . -name '*.jpg'`
`-exec convert {} -resize 50% {} \;`

Oops, you need to change '50%' to '60%'!

Without Shortcuts: Lots of arrow key navigation, or retyping it.

With Shortcuts:

1. Ctrl+R and start typing 'find'
2. Found it? Ctrl+A (jump to start), edit '50%', Enter

Power User Shortcuts

1. Clearing the Screen

* **Ctrl+L:** Clears the clutter, but doesn't delete your history. Similar to the `clear` command.

2. Instant Logout (Most Shells):

* **Ctrl+D:** Saves you typing `exit` or `logout`

Important Notes

- **Consistency is Key:** Using shortcuts regularly is what makes them truly powerful.
- **Exploration:** Your shell and terminal emulator may have even more shortcuts to discover.

Additional Resources

- **Linux command line shortcuts cheat sheet:**
  https://linuxize.com/post/bash-keyboard-shortcuts/

Up Next (Future Chapters)

- **Text Editing Within the Terminal:** Commands like nano have their own shortcuts (building upon the basics).
- **Advanced History Tricks:** Searching your history, selectively re-running parts of past commands, and more.

Practice

1. **Typo Master:** Intentionally type commands with various mistakes (wrong words, transpositions). Fix them exclusively using editing shortcuts.
2. **The History Challenge:** Use Ctrl+R and the `!prefix` tricks to re-run past commands with *zero* retyping of the actual command itself.

Customization Note

Some advanced shells let you customize your shortcuts! This can be amazing for commands you use often.

Share Your Favorites

What keyboard shortcut has become so ingrained in your command-line workflow that you couldn't function without it?

Section 3:
Illuminating File Insights

Unveiling Text Realms: Delving into the Gnome Text Editor gedit

While the Linux command line is incredibly powerful, sometimes you need a more traditional text editing experience. gedit, often the default graphical text editor in Gnome-based Linux distributions, offers a perfect blend of simplicity and features for working with your files.

Why gedit?

- **Intuitive Interface:** If you're used to text editors on Windows or Mac, gedit will feel familiar. Less mental overhead means focusing on your content.
- **Included by Default:** Many Linux distributions ship with gedit ready to go. No extra installation needed!
- **Under the Hood Power:** gedit might seem simple, but it hides features like syntax highlighting, search-and-replace, and plugins for the truly power-hungry.

Launching and Navigating gedit

1. **Graphical Way:** Often found in your applications menu under "Text Editor" or something similar.
2. **Command Line Way:** You can launch gedit from your terminal:
    - `gedit filename.txt` (Opens an existing file)
    - `gedit` (Opens a new, blank document)

The gedit Interface

Let's dissect the typical gedit window:

- **Title Bar:** Shows filename or "Untitled Document…"
- **Menu Bar:** Classic File, Edit, View, etc. We'll explore these soon.
- **Toolbar:** Buttons for common actions (New, Open, Save, Print, etc.)

- **Main Editing Area:** Where you type your text!
- **Status Bar:** Shows file information, cursor position, etc.

Core Actions

1. **New, Open, Save:** Found under "File" or the toolbar, these function as you'd expect.
2. **Cut, Copy, Paste:** "Edit" menu, usual keyboard shortcuts (Ctrl+X, Ctrl+C, Ctrl+V), or even right-click for a context menu.
3. **Undo/Redo:** Mistakes happen! 'Edit' menu or Ctrl+Z (Undo), Ctrl+Y (Redo).

Search and Replace

- **Find:** Ctrl+F opens a search bar. Find text within your document.
- **Replace:** Ctrl+H lets you find text AND replace it with something else. Use with caution!

Scenario: Fixing a Report

A coworker sends you a draft report.txt. You need to find all instances of "project alpha" and change them to the current project name.

1. Open the report in gedit
2. Ctrl+H for Replace
3. Find: "project alpha" / Replace with: "Project Zeta"
4. You can 'Replace' one at a time, or 'Replace All' for speed.

Beyond the Basics

1. **Syntax Highlighting:** Gedit automatically detects many programming languages and file formats, coloring code for readability.
2. **Preferences:** Under the 'View' menu, customize things like line numbers, highlighting the current line, and themes.
3. **Plugins:** Get serious power with plugins. To install, search for instructions specific to your distribution, but often these plugins provide:
   - Spell checking
   - Version control integration (for programmers)
   - Specialized formatting tools

Important Notes

- **Alternatives:** If gedit feels too simple, many other Linux text editors exist (Vim, Emacs, etc.). Those have a steeper learning curve, but offer unmatched power.
- **gedit is Not a Word Processor:** For fancy document layouts, consider a dedicated office suite like LibreOffice.

Additional Resources

- **Official gedit Documentation:** Consult the GNOME Project's resources: https://help.gnome.org/users/gedit/stable/gedit-plugin-guide.html.en for the most up-to-date help

Up Next: Nano

For editing files *directly within the terminal*, we'll learn the command-line text editor 'nano' – the go-to when you don't have a graphical interface.

Practice

1. **Take Notes:** Use gedit instead of a notepad app for a few days. Get used to its interface.
2. **Edit a Code File:** If you do any coding (even basic HTML), try editing it in gedit. Does it recognize the syntax?

Mastering Nano: Navigating Text Realms with the Command-Line Editor, Part 1

Nano is your lifeline when you need to edit text files directly within the terminal. Whether it's tweaking a configuration file, writing a quick script, or making notes during a remote session, Nano is the go-to for its simplicity.

Why Nano?

- **Always There:** Nano comes pre-installed on most Linux distributions. No extra setup is needed.
- **Beginner Friendly:** Minimal learning curve. Focus on editing text, not memorizing complex key combinations.
- **Shortcut Helper:** The most important commands are displayed at the bottom of the screen, so you don't have to remember them all.

Launching Nano

1. **To Edit an Existing File:** `nano filename.txt`
2. **To Start a New File:** `nano` (You'll be asked for a filename when saving)

The Nano Interface

- **Title Bar:** Shows the filename (or 'New Buffer')
- **Editing Area:** This is where you type your text.
- **Shortcut Bar:** Provides a constant reminder of the most essential commands.

Basic Navigation

- **Arrow Keys:** Move around the file one character or one line at a time.
- **Page Up/Page Down:** Jump up or down a full screen of text.
- **Home/End:** Jump to the beginning/end of the current line
- **Ctrl+_ (Ctrl + Underscore):** Go to a specific line number

Editing Text

- **Typing Works!:** Nano functions like a very basic text editor. Type to insert text, Backspace to delete.
- **No Mouse by Default:** Get used to keyboard-based editing. You *can* configure mouse support if you desperately need it.

Saving Your Work (Important!)

- **Ctrl+O** (The letter 'O') : This is the 'Write Out' command to save. It will prompt you for a filename if the file is new.
- **Ctrl+X:** Exits Nano. It will ask you if you want to save changes if you haven't already.

Scenario: Editing a Configuration File

Imagine you need to modify a system setting stored in /etc/network.conf.

1. **Launch:** sudo nano /etc/network.conf ('sudo' may be needed for system files)
2. **Navigate:** Use arrows, Page Up/Down etc., to find the line to change.
3. **Edit:** Modify the text carefully!
4. **Save:** Ctrl+O, then Enter to confirm the filename.
5. **Exit:** Ctrl +X

Core Shortcuts (You'll Use These A Lot)

- **Ctrl+G:** Get help (more on this later)
- **Ctrl+O:** Save ('Write Out')
- **Ctrl+X:** Exit
- **Ctrl+W:** Search for text ('Where Is')

Beyond the Basics

- **Cut and Paste:**
  - Ctrl+K: 'Cut' the current line
  - Ctrl+U: 'Uncut' (paste) the cut line where your cursor is
- **Word at a time:**
  - Ctrl+Space: Move forward one word
  - Alt+Space: Move backwards one word

Note: Some features might be slightly different between Nano versions.

Additional Resources

- **The Nano Help Page:** Press Ctrl+G within Nano for the official help
- **Nano Cheat Sheet:**
  https://www.nano-editor.org/dist/latest/cheatsheet.html

Up Next: Part 2

- **Search-and-replace functionality**
- More advanced editing (copying blocks of text, etc.)
- Customization (if your Nano supports it)

Practice

1. **Nano Diary:** Instead of notes on paper, write a few paragraphs in Nano each day. This forces you to use navigation shortcuts.
2. **Fix a Config (Carefully!):** If you're comfortable, try editing a NON-CRITICAL configuration file on your system. Start small, like changing a program's color scheme if its settings are text-based. Always have a backup plan!

Nano vs. gedit vs. The Big Guns

- **gedit:** For when you need a traditional text editor experience *with* graphical interface.
- **Nano:** When working exclusively within the terminal
- **Vim/Emacs:** Immensely powerful, but notoriously complex. Great if you plan to invest serious time into learning them, overkill for basic edits.

Share Your Nano Discoveries!

Do you have some Nano tricks up your sleeve that make your life easier?

Mastering Nano: Navigating Text Realms with the Command-Line Editor, Part 2

In this chapter, we'll move beyond basic editing and discover search-and-replace, more advanced techniques, and even how to slightly customize Nano's behavior.

Harnessing Search (and Replace) Power

1. **Finding Text:**
   - Ctrl+W ('Where is'): Opens the search prompt.
   - Type your search term, and hit Enter. Nano will jump to the next match.
   - Keep hitting Enter to cycle through matches.
2. **Replace Mode:**
   - Alt+R (Meta+R on some systems): Toggles replace mode
   - Search for a string
   - You'll be asked what to replace it with.
   - Options:
     - Type the replacement, Enter to replace the *current* match
     - Press 'A' to replace ALL matches from that point onwards
     - 'N' to skip the current match

Scenario: Configuration Updates

You must change an IP address that appears multiple times in a config file.

1. Open the file with Nano.
2. Ctrl+W, search for the old IP address
3. Alt+R to enable Replace mode
4. Type the new IP address, then carefully choose between Enter (replace only that instance) or 'A' (replace all).

Advanced Editing: Blocks of Text

Nano lets you manipulate text in chunks:

- **Marking Begins:**
  - Ctrl+^ (Hold Ctrl and press the '6' key) This sets a 'mark' at your cursor position.
- **Selecting a Block:**

- Move your cursor. Everything between the 'mark' and your current position becomes highlighted.
- **Actions on a Block:**
  - Ctrl+K to 'cut' the marked text.
  - Ctrl+U to 'uncut' (paste) it at your current cursor location.

Power User: Copying Without Cutting

- Alt+^ (Alt + '6'): Copies the selected block of text, leaving the original intact. (Note: Not all Nano versions support this)

Customizing Nano (If Supported)

Some options you might be able to change:

- **Turn On Line Numbers:** Great for referencing code. Look for a ~/.nanorc file (or create one) and add the line 'set linenumbers'
- **Syntax Highlighting:** If supported, Nano can try to color code based on file type. This requires configuration within your .nanorc file
- **Mouse Support:** For die-hard mouse lovers, consider adding 'set mouse' if your version of Nano supports it.

Important:

- **Nano Versions Matter:** Not all versions of Nano have the same features.
- **Config File:** Customizations are often done by editing a file called .nanorc in your home directory. Search online for instructions specifically for your Linux distribution.

Additional Resources

- **Nano's Built-in Help:** Always remember Ctrl+G to access the official help screen for a refresher.
- **Customizing Nano:**
  https://www.nano-editor.org/dist/latest/nanorc.5.html

Up Next (Future Chapters)

- **Command-Line History:** How to recall, edit, and re-use past commands to save serious typing.
- **The 'less' Command:** A powerful way to navigate through text files with even more features than Nano's built-in viewing.

Practice

1. **The Great Text Edit:** Find a text file (code, config, anything). Intentionally introduce small errors (typos, extra lines). Now fix ONLY using Nano's search, replace, and block editing.
2. (Advanced): **Nano Config Hunt:** Does your version of Nano support customization? Explore online, try editing a `.nanorc` file, and see if you can change a setting.

Caution With Replace!

Replace mode is powerful but can be dangerous if you're not careful. It's often wise to search through a few matches manually before doing a global 'replace all'. Prevention is better than fixing a mess!

Your Nano Workflow

How do you use Nano? Are you a minimalist, getting in and out for quick edits? Or do you take advantage of its features for longer text work sessions?

Tracing Your Steps: Unveiling Command-Line History, Part 1

The Linux command line remembers your past actions! This isn't just for nostalgia—your command history is a powerful tool to save time, uncover patterns, and even automate tasks.

Why Command History Matters

1. **Less Retyping:** Ever need to re-run an earlier command? History makes it lightning-fast to recall, saving precious keystrokes.
2. **Fix and Retry:** Did a complex command have a typo? Easily find it, fix the mistake, and try again.
3. **Pattern Recognition:** Command history reveals your habits. Which commands do you use most? This can lead to optimizing your workflow.
4. **Automate the Frequent:** Tasks you often run manually could potentially be turned into scripts or aliases (future chapters!).

Basic Tools of the Trade

1. **The Up/Down Arrows:** Your first line of defense. Cycle backwards and forwards through recent commands.
2. **Ctrl+R (Reverse Search):** Start typing part of a past command, and the shell will try to find a match in your history. Keep hitting Ctrl+R to cycle matches if there are multiple.
3. **The `history` Command:** Used on its own, it dumps a numbered list of your past commands to the screen. Can be quite long on well-used systems!

Scenario 1: The Long-Lost Command

You ran a command a few days ago to configure network settings. It was complex, and you don't quite remember the exact options you used.

- **Solution:**
  - Ctrl+R and start typing fragments you remember ("network," an IP address, etc.)
  - Or, `history | grep network` (More on 'grep' later, but this searches your history)

Scenario 2: Fixing Mistakes

You mistyped a long command with `rm` (delete). Thankfully, you didn't execute it yet!

- **Solution:**
    - ○ Up arrow to find it, edit carefully, then re-run.

Beyond the Basics

- **History is Customizable:** Most shells let you control how many commands are stored. Search "[Your shell name] history settings" for how to adjust this.
- **Selective Execution:**
    - ○ `!245` : Re-runs the command numbered 245 in your `history` list.
    - ○ `!-3` : Re-runs the command from three commands ago.

Important Notes

- **Privacy:** Your history is generally stored in a file. If others share your computer, sensitive commands might be visible.
- **Shells Matter:** Different shells (Bash, Zsh, etc.) might have slightly different history features.

Additional Resources

- **'history' Command Manual:**
  https://www.gnu.org/software/bash/manual/html_node/Bash-History-Buil tins.html

Up Next: Part 2

- **Filtering history for powerful searches**
- **Reusing parts of old commands, not just the entire thing**
- **Security aspects of command history**

Practice

1. **Intentional Typos:** Type a few long-ish commands (try `ls -alR /`, etc.). Now intentionally add typos, then use history tools to fix them quickly.
2. **History Hunt:** Use Ctrl+R or the `history` command to answer these:
    - ○ When was the last time you changed your password? (Search for 'passwd').

○ What image editing commands have you used in the past week?

Pro Tip

Try adding the command `history` to the end of your shell prompt. This way, a few recent commands are always visible at a glance! (How to do this depends on your shell)

Share Your History Tricks

Do you have clever ways of searching through your command history or reusing old commands?

Tracing Your Steps: Unveiling Command-Line History, Part 2

Let's dive deeper into how the command line lets you search, manipulate, and learn from your past actions, boosting your efficiency.

Command-Line Detective: Filtering with 'grep'

- **Problem:** The history command alone can be overwhelming. How do you find that *one* command you used last month related to image processing?
- **Solution:** 'grep'! It searches for text patterns. Pipe your history through it:

  history | grep imagemagick (Assuming 'imagemagick' was part of the command)

Scenario: Troubleshooting Time

A website configuration change you made a while back seems to have caused errors. You can't remember exactly what you did.

1. history | grep apache (Or the name of your web server software) to narrow down commands.
2. Spot a likely culprit? Use the !number trick to re-run the command to investigate further, then fix it.

Reusing Parts of Old Commands

Sometimes you *almost* want to rerun a past command, but need to change a little piece.

- **The 'Bang' Shortcuts:**
  - !!:s/old/new/ : Takes your previous command and replaces "old" with "new".
  - !*: All the arguments from your previous command, ready to be appended to a new one.

Example:

1. You run: ping 8.8.8.8 (To test network connectivity)

2. Want to ping a different address? `ping !*` reuses it, so you just type `ping 1.1.1.1`

Controlling History

- **Temporarily Disable:** If you're doing sensitive work, prepend a command with a space. Most shells won't save it to history this way.
- **Instant Erase:** The `history -c` command wipes your history clean.
- **Selective Deletion:** `history -d 623` (deletes line 623). Use the `history` command, find the line number, then remove it.

Security Considerations

- **Plaintext Storage:** By default, your history is often a text file (`~/.bash_history` being common). Someone with access to your computer could see it.
- **Solutions (if needed):**
  - Encryption of your home directory can help.
  - Clearing history regularly with `history -c`
  - Some shells have settings to avoid logging sensitive commands

Advanced: History Within Scripts

Shells like Bash allow scripts to access command history. This lets you write sophisticated automation tools! (This is a complex topic, so start with these searches if you're interested):

- "Bash history expansion in scripts"
- "Using command history for automation"

Additional Resources

- **The Power of grep:**
  https://www.gnu.org/software/grep/manual/grep.html

Up Next (Future Chapters)

- **The 'less' Command:** For navigating large files *and* your history when simple scrolling isn't enough.
- **Automating with history:** The foundation for turning frequent command sequences into scripts or aliases

Practice

1. **The Mystery Edit:** Intentionally change a text file. Now, use `history` and `grep` to figure out which command you used, and which file you modified.
2. **Practice 'Bang' (!):**
   - Run `ls -l /usr/bin`
   - Now, `mkdir !*` What did this do? (Carefully!)

Caution

- History manipulation is powerful. Always double-check, especially with `!` tricks, before you re-run a modified command. Prevention beats fixing unintended consequences!

Share Your History Wisdom

Do you have a favorite way to search your history, or some clever use of it for automation?

Exploring Text Dynamics: Navigating Files with the 'less' Command, Part 1

If you need to view a file in the terminal, 'less' is your far more capable companion compared to basic commands like 'cat'. It empowers you to move through text gracefully, search for patterns, and uncover insights within your files.

Why 'less' Is More

- **Handles Large Files:** 'cat' dumps everything to the screen at once, overwhelming for big files. 'less' shows it page-by-page.
- **Controlled Navigation:** Arrows, Page Up/Down… move through text at your own pace, not the way the file dictates.
- **Search Functionality** Find specific words or patterns – invaluable when digging through logs or config files.

Basic Usage

Viewing a File:
```
less filename.txt
```

1.
2. **Navigation (Inside 'less')**
    - **Arrows:** Line by line movement
    - **Page Up/Page Down:** Jump full screens
    - **Spacebar:** Jump one screen down
    - **G / g :** Go to the end / start of the file
3. **Searching:**
    - **/pattern ** (Forward search): Finds the next occurrence of "pattern"
    - **?pattern ** (Backward search): Finds the previous occurrence
4. **Exiting 'less':** Press 'q'

Scenario 1: Log Analysis

A web server is acting up. You suspect the error log might hold clues:

1. `less /var/log/apache/error.log` (path might vary)
2. `/Server Error` : Search for relevant lines
3. Use 'n' (lowercase) to cycle between search matches to investigate

Scenario 2: Reading Man Pages

Manuals for commands often use 'less' for display:

1. `man ls` : To view the manual for the 'ls' command
2. Navigation and search within 'less' helps you find the specific option you need

Core Commands (Inside 'less')

- **n:** Next search match
- **N:** Previous search match
- **h:** Show a 'help' screen of less commands
- **q:** Quit

Beyond the Basics

- **Line Numbers:** Press '-N' (shift + N) to toggle line numbers, great for referencing code or config files
- **Following Changes:** The '-F' option forces 'less' to keep the view at the end of the file and update as the file grows. Handy for real-time monitoring of logs.
- **Multiple Files:** `less file1.txt file2.log` ... lets you open multiple files, and easily switch between them.

Important Notes

- **Read-Only:** 'less' is for *viewing*. You'll need a text editor (like Nano) to make changes.
- **Customizations:** Some advanced features of 'less' are customizable, search for things like "lesspipe" and "lesskey" if you want to fine-tune its behavior.

Additional Resources

- **The 'less' man page:** Type `man less` right in your terminal for the official reference

Up Next: Part 2

- **More advanced search techniques within 'less'**
- **Using 'less' to view the output of other commands (piping)**
- **Troubleshooting common issues with 'less'**

Practice

1. **Examine a Config File:** Find a system configuration file (be careful not to change it!) Use 'less' to navigate and search within it.
2. **Read Your History:** `less ~/.bash_history` – Explore your past commands! Can you find patterns in what you used frequently?

Pro Tip: 'less' as a Filter

Pipe any command with lots of output into 'less' for easier reading. Example: `ps aux | less` (lists processes)

Share Your 'less' Discoveries

Do you have a neat way you use 'less', perhaps in combination with other commands for clever analysis?

Exploring Text Dynamics: Navigating Files with the 'less' Command, Part 2

Let's dive deeper into the advanced features of 'less', transforming you from casual reader to skilled text file navigator.

Mastering Search Within 'less'

- **Regular Expressions (Advanced):** 'less' supports regular expressions, a powerful pattern-matching language. (Search online for "Linux regular expressions" for a primer)
- **Case Sensitivity:**
    - `/pattern` – Case-sensitive search
    - `-i /pattern` – Forces case-insensitive search

Scenario: Code Troubleshooting

You're debugging code with error messages sprinkled through a log file.

1. `less error.log`
2. `-i /errorcode543` : Search for the specific code, ignoring case.
3. Use 'n' and 'N' to cycle between matches

Beyond Basic Navigation

- **Bookmarks:**
    1. Press 'm' followed by a letter (like 'a') to place a mark.
    2. Press " (single quote) followed by a letter (like 'a') to jump back to that mark. Great for comparing distant sections of a file.
- **Follow Mode + Search:** Combo move!
    1. `-F`: Enter Follow mode (like 'tail -f')
    2. Press / to search while staying up-to-date with the latest changes.

Filtering and Pipes

'less' can be part of a command chain using pipes ('|').

- **Scenario: Finding the Big Files**
    - `ls -lS | less` - Lists files ordered by size, feeding the output into 'less' for controlled viewing.

- **Pre-processors with 'lesspipe':** If your distribution supports it, 'lesspipe' lets 'less' handle various file formats (ZIP contents, etc.). Search for instructions related to your Linux distribution .

Troubleshooting 'less'

- **Odd characters on screen:** Check if your terminal emulator's character encoding matches the file you're viewing.
- **Features Not Working:** Older 'less' versions may lack some features. See if a newer version is available.
- **When in Doubt: The Man Page:** `man less` is your friend

Additional Resources

- **'less' FAQ** (https://www.greenwoodsoftware.com/less/faq.html

Up Next (Future Chapters)

- **The 'cat' and 'tac' Commands:** Simple text viewing with a twist.
- **'head' and 'tail':** When you only need the beginning or end of a file.
- **Text Analytics with 'wc'** Counting characters, words, and lines

Practice

1. **A Text Adventure:** Find a public domain text file of a book. Load it in 'less', then:
   - Search for the main character's name
   - Use bookmarks to jump between important scenes
2. **System Sleuth:** `dmesg | less` (might need 'sudo') to view kernel logs. Try searching for the name of your network card or hard drive.

Pro Tip: Combining Search and Follow

While in 'Follow' mode (-F), start a search. As new text matching the search appears at the bottom of the file, it's automatically highlighted!

Share Your 'less' Workflow

How does 'less' fit into your regular file analysis work? Do you use it with other commands for powerful filtering?

Decoding File Realities: Insightful Analysis with the cat and tac Commands, Part 1

While seemingly simple, the 'cat' and 'tac' commands hold surprising power for text file exploration within the Linux command line.

What are 'cat' and 'tac'?

- **cat (concatenate):** The classic. Dumps the entire contents of files to your screen.
- **tac:** 'cat' in reverse! Shows files with the last line at the top, first line at the bottom.

Basic Usage

1. **Viewing a File:**
   - `cat mytextfile.txt`
2. **Concatenating Multiple Files:**
   - `cat file1.log file2.log > combinedlog.txt` (Merges them into a new file)

Scenario 1: Quick Error Check

A script is misbehaving. You suspect the most recent log entry holds the key.

1. `tac errors.log` (Shows the last entries first)

Scenario 2: Combining Configs

You need to merge pieces from multiple configuration files into a master file.

1. `cat settings1.conf settings2.conf > master_config.conf`

Beyond the Obvious

- **Piping into Others:**
  - `cat systeminfo.txt | less` (Use 'less' for controlled navigation of large output).

- `cat imagelist.txt | grep .jpg` (Filter out only lines containing ".jpg")
- **Redirects ('<' and '>'):**
    - `cat < existingfile.txt > copy_of_file.txt` (Makes a quick copy)
    - `cat > newfile.txt` (Type some text, press Ctrl+D to end input and save)

'cat' for Cautious Analysis

- **Preserves File:** 'cat' is read-only, a safety net when examining important files.
- **Fast:** Dumps everything at once. Ideal for quick glances or piping into other filtering commands.
- **Handles (Almost) Anything:** Text files, code, even some binary data (though the output might look garbled).

'tac' for Reverse Logic

- **Troubleshooting: Bottom-up reveals the *latest* events in logs.
- **Finding Patterns at the End:** Some logs put summary lines at the bottom, 'tac' makes those visible first.

Important Notes

- **Large Files = Trouble:** `cat` on a huge file floods your screen! Use 'less', 'head,' or 'tail' instead.
- **Binary Data:** `cat` can try to display images, PDFs, etc., but will result in terminal chaos. Use the `file` command first to identify file types

Up Next: Part 2

- **Creative 'cat' combinations for filtering and transformations**
- **'tac' tricks for unusual file analysis**
- **Situations where 'cat' and 'tac' might NOT be the best tools**

Practice

1. **Reverse Engineering:** Have a short script? `tac` its output while running it, sometimes odd patterns at the *end* reveal errors.
2. **Compress and Read:** If you have a .gz log file:
    - `zcat logfile.gz | less` (Decompress on the fly)

Pro Tip: Numbering Lines

Combine 'cat' with 'nl' to add line numbers to output:

- `cat -n todo_list.txt`

Share Your 'cat' / 'tac' combos

Do you have a clever way you use these commands in conjunction with others for extracting specific information?

Decoding File Realities: Insightful Analysis with the cat and tac Commands, Part 2

Let's harness the power of these deceptively simple tools for file manipulation and information extraction.

Clever 'cat' Combos

1. **Quick Difference Check:**
   - `cat file1.txt file2.txt > combined.txt`
   - `diff combined.txt file1.txt` (The 'diff' command shows differences line-by-line)
2. **Appending Data:**
   - `cat extra_info.txt >> existing_log.txt` (Adds content to the end of a file)
3. **Selective Filtering with 'grep':**
   - `cat system.log | grep 'error'` Shows only lines with the word "error"

Scenario: Troubleshooting, but Nicely

A website misbehaves, the relevant log is *huge*. You need error lines, but don't want to flood your screen.

1. `cat webserver.log | grep 'error' > errors_only.txt`
2. `less errors_only.txt` (Now you analyze with control)

'tac' Tricks

1. **Progress Reports in Reverse:** Some installers log to a file. Run `tac install.log | less` and keep the '-F' (Follow) mode of 'less' on to see the *newest* install output update live.
2. **Breaking Down Changes:**
   If you frequently modify a config file:
   - `cp config.txt config.txt.old` (Make a backup)
   - Make your edits to 'config.txt'
   - `tac config.txt.old config.txt | less` (shows differences, most recent first)

When 'cat' and 'tac' Aren't Enough

- **Huge Files:** 'head' and 'tail' are your friends for peeking at beginnings / ends.
- **Structured Data:** CSV files, complex XML, etc., need specialized tools. Search "linux command line parse CSV" for guides (often involving 'awk' or 'cut').
- **Binary Files:** 'cat' will try but cause chaos. Tools like 'strings' attempt to extract readable text from within binary data.

Important Notes

- **Redirects are Powerful:** Use '>' with care or you risk overwriting files!
- **Permissions Matter:** If you can't 'cat' a file, you might lack read permissions. Sometimes you'll need 'sudo' for system files

Additional Resources

- **GNU Core Utilities: 'cat' and 'tac' man pages:** (https://www.gnu.org/software/coreutils/manual/)

Up Next (Future Chapters)

- **'head' and 'tail':** Extracting the beginnings and ends of files
- **Word and Character Counting ('wc'):** Simple analytics on your text data

Practice

1. **Change Detective:**
   - Find a text file you modify occasionally.
   - Make a copy. Now modify the original, make note of what you changed
   - `tac` both versions through `diff` or in 'less'. Can you spot your edits?
2. **Log Rotation in Reverse:**
   - Many systems rotate logs (log.1, log.2, etc., oldest one deleted). 'tac' the numbered logs in *ascending* order, then pipe into 'less' to have a continuous log view

Caution: `cat something.txt > something.txt` **Empties a file!** The redirect overwrites the original. Always double-check before using '>'

Capturing Text Essence: Harnessing the Power of head and tail Commands, Part 1

Learn to efficiently slice and dice text files, revealing the information you need from the beginning or end.

Why 'head' and 'tail'?

- **Speed:** When you only care about a file's start or end, these commands are *far* faster than loading the entire thing in an editor.
- **Massive Files:** 'head' and 'tail' work on files too large for some text editors to handle.
- **Automation:** They're perfect components within scripts for log monitoring or data processing tasks.

Basic Usage

1. **'head': Top Lines**
   - `head filename.txt` (Shows the first 10 lines by default)
   - `head -n 20 filename.txt` (Shows the first 20 lines)
2. **'tail': Bottom Lines**
   - `tail filename.txt` (Shows the last 10 lines)
   - `tail -n 30 filename.txt` (Shows the last 30 lines)

Scenario 1: Quick Check

You've modified a config file. Want to make sure your changes are at the end as expected:

- `tail -n 5 config.txt` (See the last 5 lines)

Scenario 2: Live Monitoring

A program outputs to a log file. You want to see the latest entries in real-time:

- `tail -f logfile.txt` ('-f' enables the follow mode)

Core Options

- **'-n' Number of Lines:** You've seen this used already

- **'-c' Number of Bytes:** For ultra-fine control, or with binary files where lines don't make sense. Example: `tail -c 100 somefile.dat`

'Follow Mode' Power (-f)

'tail -f' is incredibly useful:

- **Troubleshooting:** Watch errors appear live within log files
- **Progress:** Monitor scripts that append to a progress report file.
- **Pipes!** Works beautifully with filtering: `tail -f errors.log | grep 'critical'`

Important Notes

- **Large Files & '-f':** If a huge file exists before you use 'tail -f' on it, you'll get the very END. To truly start monitoring new additions, try: `tail -f logfile.txt -n 0`
- **Permissions:** Just like 'cat', if you lack read permissions on a file, 'head' and 'tail' won't work.

Additional Resources

- **The 'head' and 'tail' man pages:** Right on your system using man head or man tail for all the details

Up Next: Part 2

- **More advanced uses of 'head' and 'tail** with pipes and filtering'
- **Combining 'head' / 'tail' for extracting middle portions of files**
- **Potential errors and how to troubleshoot them**

Practice

1. **Excerpt a Poem:** Find a public domain text file of a poem. Use 'head' and 'tail' to isolate a few stanzas.
2. **Compress and Peek:** If you have a .zip file:
   - `unzip -l zipfile.zip | tail` (lists the last few files in the archive)

Pro Tip: Headless 'head'

Pipe lengthy command output into 'head' to limit it on the screen:

`ps aux | head -n 15` (Shows only the top 15 processes)

Share Your 'head' / 'tail' Tricks

Do you use these commands in clever ways, especially when combined with other tools? Let's learn from each other!

Capturing Text Essence: Harnessing the Power of head and tail Commands, Part 2

Let's continue our text-taming adventure with "Capturing Text Essence: Harnessing the Power of head and tail Commands, Part 2"! We'll wield 'head' and 'tail' in conjunction with other tools to become masters of file analysis.

Pipes and Filtering: The Combo Move

1. **Isolating Issues:**
   - `tail -n 30 error.log | grep '\[error\]'` Shows only the last 30 lines of the log containing the word "error"
2. **First Bytes:**
   - `head -c 20 some_document.pdf | file -` Feeds the first 20 bytes to the 'file' command to figure out the file type (even if misnamed!)

Scenario: Troubleshooting, Large Log

A huge log file is slowing down your text editor. You suspect the relevant problems are recent:

1. `tail -n 5000 errors.log > recent_errors.log` (Isolate a manageable chunk)
2. `less recent_errors.log` (Analyze with control)

Slicing the Middle (Tricky but Powerful)

1. **Lines 20-30:**
   - `head -n 30 bigfile.txt | tail -n 10` (Get first 30 lines, *then* grab the last 10 of those)
2. **Bytes Trick (Advanced):** If you know the size, use 'dd' for ultra-precise extraction. Search for "linux dd command extract part of file" for tutorials (this gets complex!)

Monitoring Progress

Imagine a script outputs this over time:

Processed 10 files...
Processed 25 files…

- `tail -f progress.log | grep 'Processed'` Shows those lines as they appear

Troubleshooting 'head' and 'tail'

- **Strange Characters:** Check your terminal's character encoding matches the file you're viewing.
- **Empty Output:** Be sure the file exists, and that you have permission to read it.
- **Old 'tail' Versions:** Older 'tail' implementations might lack modern features.

Additional Resources

- **Power User Filtering:** Learn about 'grep', 'sed', and 'awk' to supercharge text analysis: (https://www.gnu.org/software/gawk/manual/gawk.html)

Up Next (Future Chapters)

- **Counting Words and Lines with 'wc'**
- **Beyond Text:** Where 'head' and 'tail' can be surprisingly useful with binary data.

Practice

1. **Real-World Scenario:** If your system has them, examine logs in `/var/log`. Look for things like kernel messages (search for 'dmesg'). Try using 'head' / 'tail' combined with 'grep' to pinpoint something interesting.
2. **Compression Power:**
   - `zcat somefile.txt.gz | tail -n 10` (Views the end of a compressed text file without decompressing the whole thing)

Watch Out: Pipes and Redirects

- `some_command | head -n 10 > output.txt` This works! Saves first 10 lines of command output.

- `head -n 10 some_file.txt > some_file.txt` **Danger!** You've overwritten the input file with an empty one.

Share Your 'head' / 'tail' Workflow

How do you integrate these commands within your regular file analysis work? Do you have scripts built around them?

Counting Characters: Mastering Text Analytics with the wc Command, Part 1

The 'wc' command (short for "word count") is a deceptively powerful tool for analyzing your text-based files.

Basic Usage

1. **Lines, Words, and Characters:**
   - `wc mydocument.txt` (Outputs all three counts)

Example Output:
100 543 3214 mydocument.txt

2.
   - 100 lines
   - 543 words
   - 3214 characters (including spaces and punctuation)
3. **Specific Counts:**
   - `wc -l mydocument.txt` (Lines only)
   - `wc -w mydocument.txt` (Words only)
   - `wc -c mydocument.txt` (Characters only)

Scenario 1: Quick Draft Check

You've written a blog post draft. A quick word count ensures you're within the website's guidelines:

- `wc -w draft.txt`

Scenario 2: Code Complexity

While not foolproof, lines-of-code can be a *rough* indicator of complexity.

- `wc -l *.py` (Counts lines in all your Python scripts)

How 'wc' Defines a "Word"

Simply put, 'wc' considers a word to be any sequence of characters separated by spaces, tabs, or newline characters.

Important Notes

- **Text Encoding Matters:** 'wc' mostly works with plain text. Odd results with some Unicode characters are possible depending on your settings.
- **Binary Data:** 'wc' will *try* to count things in binary files, but the results, especially word counts, will often be meaningless.

Additional Resources

- **Exploring 'wc' options:** The manual page (man wc) for details

Up Next: Part 2

- **Counting within selections of text, not just whole files**
- **Using 'wc' in conjunction with other commands for filtering**
- **Potential issues with 'wc' and how to handle them**

Practice

1. **Poem Analysis:** Find a public domain poem online.
   - How does the words-per-line ratio change throughout? (Use 'wc -l' and 'wc -w' on individual lines by piping into 'wc')
2. **Log Verbosity:** If you have system logs, try wc -l on them over different time periods (use 'head' and 'tail' to grab slices). Does the number of log lines correlate with periods of system activity?

Pro Tip: Counting More than Lines

While 'wc -l' is obvious, remember these:

- `grep 'searchterm' somefile.txt | wc -l` (Counts lines *matching* your search)
- `find . -name '*.jpg' | wc -l` (Counts how many JPG images are within a directory tree)

Share Your 'wc' Use Cases

Do you use 'wc' in any unique ways for file analysis? Maybe in scripts to check if output meets certain size expectations?

Counting Characters: Mastering Text Analytics with the wc Command, Part 2

Welcome to "Counting Characters: Mastering Text Analytics with the wc Command, Part 2"! Let's dive deeper into the power of 'wc' for extracting insights from your text files.

Counting Within Selections

'wc' doesn't have to work on *whole* files. Let's combine it with other tools:

1. **Lines Containing a Word:**
   - `grep 'important_topic' report.txt | wc -l` (Tells you how often that topic is mentioned)
2. **Characters in a Specific Column:**
   - `cut -c 10-20 datafile.csv | wc -c` (Extracts characters from columns 10 to 20, then counts them. 'cut' is a column-slicing tool)

Scenario: Analyzing Survey Data

You have a CSV with survey responses. You need a quick feel for how long (in characters) the comments are:

1. `head -n 2 survey.csv` (Examine the first two lines to figure out which column number contains the comments)
2. `cut -c 42- survey.csv | wc -c` (Assuming comments are in column 42 and onward, extract that data and count)

'wc' Pitfalls and Workarounds

- **Unicode Quirks:** Very complex text encoding might cause 'wc' to slightly miscount characters. Advanced text analysis tools often handle this better.
- **'wc' is Tricked by Formatting:** If a file has hidden formatting codes (like in some Word documents), 'wc' will count those, not just the visible text. Solutions:
   - Save as plain text first
   - Use specialized file type converters (search for things like "convert Word doc to plain text linux")

Additional Resources

- **Beyond Basic Text Analysis:** Explore tools like 'awk' and 'sed' for powerful text manipulation on the command line

Practice

1. **Log Changes:** If you have system logs from different days:
   - Use 'wc -l' on each. Do log sizes correlate to system events you know occurred?
2. **Code Evolution:** If you have version control (like Git), get a word count for different historical revisions of a code file. Does it track with how features were added over time?

Caution: Interpretation

Bigger word counts don't always equal better! Metrics from 'wc' are a *starting point* for analysis, not the whole story.

Section 4:
Empowering Command Prowess

Command Chronicles: Exploring Command Categories and Functions, Part 1

Understanding the different types of commands you encounter in the Linux world is key to building your mental map of the terminal landscape.

Types of Commands

1. **Built-in Shell Commands:** These are part of the shell itself (like Bash). Examples:
   - cd (Change directory)
   - pwd (Print current directory)
   - echo (Print text to the screen)
   - history (Shows your command history)
2. **Executable Programs:** Individual files that live on your file system. Examples:
   - ls (List files)
   - grep (Search for text patterns)
   - nano (If installed, it's a text editor)
   - Thousands more depending on what you've installed!

Why Does This Distinction Matter?

- **Troubleshooting Help:** Knowing the difference helps you find the right help resources (shell manual vs. command-specific manuals)
- **Environment and Paths:** Built-ins always work. Executables need to be in a location your shell knows as part of your PATH variable (more on that in later chapters)
- **Customization:** Shells are heavily customizable, and so are some individual programs, but in different ways.

Scenario: "Command Not Found"

You try to run `cool_program`. Error: "command not found". Possible reasons:

- **Typo:** Double-check!
- **Not Installed:** You might need to install it using your Linux distribution's package manager.
- **Wrong Path:** If it's installed, but not in a standard location, you'll need the full path (e.g., `/home/yourname/somefolder/cool_program`)

How to Tell the Difference

1. **The `which` Command:**
   - `which ls` : Tells you where 'ls' is found, meaning it's an executable
   - `which cd` : Likely no results, meaning 'cd' is a shell built-in
2. **The `type` Command:**
   - `type ls` : Outputs 'ls is hashed...' (indicating executable)
   - `type cd` : Outputs 'cd is a shell builtin'

Important Notes

- **Shells Matter:** Different shells (Bash, Zsh, etc.) have slightly different built-in command sets. Most basics are the same, though.
- **Complexity is Hidden:** Some things seem like built-ins, but are secretly tiny programs for convenience. This gets into advanced shell details.

Additional Resources

- **Your Shell's Manual:** Using `man bash` (if you use Bash) will have a section on built-in commands
- **Exploring Standard Paths:**
  https://www.linuxtopia.org/online_books/linux_beginner_books/linux_file_system/linux_07_FileSystemHierarchy.html

Up Next: Part 2

- **Common command categories** (file manipulation, text processing, system info...)
- **Finding detailed information about commands** (man, `--help`, etc.)

- **What happens when you type a command and hit Enter?** (A peek behind the scenes)

Practice

1. **Pick 5 Commands:** Use `which` or `type` to see if they're built-in or executables.
2. **Mystery Command:** Find a command you've never used. What category does it *seem* to fall into? We'll cover how to find out for sure in the next part!

Share Your Insights

Do you have a mental 'map' of command types you find useful? Are there any commands that still surprise you with whether they're built-in or not?

Command Chronicles: Exploring Command Categories and Functions, Part 2

Welcome to "Command Chronicles: Exploring Command Categories and Functions, Part 2"! Let's organize the vast landscape of Linux commands to speed up your terminal navigation.

Common Command Categories

1. **File Manipulation:** The workhorses of your toolbox
   - cp, mv, rm, mkdir: Copying, moving, deleting, creating directories
   - touch: Updating timestamps
   - find: Powerful search based on various criteria
2. **Text Processing:** Where things get interesting
   - grep: The search maestro
   - sed: Stream editor for text transformations
   - awk: A mini programming language for text manipulation
   - cut, sort, uniq: Slicing, sorting, and finding unique lines
3. **System Information:** Know the state of your machine
   - top or htop: Live view of processes
   - df: Disk space usage
   - free : Memory usage
   - uptime: How long the system has been running
4. **System Administration:** (Often needs 'sudo' or root privileges)
   - useradd, usermod: Managing user accounts
   - apt-get or yum (depending on your Linux distribution): Package management
   - service or systemctl: Controlling system services
5. **Compression and Archiving:**
   - zip, unzip
   - tar
   - gzip, bzip2
6. **Network Tools:**
   - ping: Test connectivity

    ◦ `ifconfig` or `ip`: Network interface details

    ◦ `curl` or `wget`: Downloading files from the web

Finding the Details

- **Man Pages:** Your ultimate reference. `man command_name` (Example: `man ls`)
- **Command's '–help':** Many commands have a short help summary built-in. Example: `ls --help`
- **Online Resources:** Tons of websites and wikis explain common Linux commands.

Scenario: The Case of the Full Filesystem

Your hard drive is filling up! Command categories to the rescue:

1. **System Info:** `df -h` shows disk usage in a human-readable format
2. **File Manipulation:** `find / -type f -size +1G` finds huge files (be careful running commands you find online!)
3. **Sorting Output:** `du -sh * | sort -h` can reveal unusually large directories.

'What Happens When I Hit Enter?' (A Simplified View)

1. **The Shell Interprets:** It breaks down your input into a command and arguments.
2. **Built-in Check:** Is the command a shell built-in function? If so, execute it directly.
3. **Path Search:** The shell looks through directories in your PATH environment variable for an executable with the same name.
4. **Execution:** The found program runs (if permissions allow it).

Important Notes

- **Category Overlap:** Some commands fit in multiple places (is 'cat' file manipulation or text processing?)
- **Distributions Matter:** Not every Linux has the exact same set of commands installed by default.

Additional Resources

- **Cheat Sheet:** https://linuxize.com/post/linux-command-line-cheat-sheet/

Up Next (Future Chapters)

- **Navigating the maze of executables (where they live, file permissions)**
- **Unlocking the power of help systems: `man`, `--help`, and more**

Practice

1. **Mystery Commands:** Pick 3 commands you rarely use. Try just their `--help` output. Can you infer their general category?
2. **Process Explorer:** Run `top` or `htop`. What category do MOST of the listed commands seem to fall into?

Caution

Especially when running commands found online, understand what they do before executing! Experimenting on a less critical system is wise.

Share Your Category System

Do you have mnemonics or ways you mentally group commands?

Navigating Executables: Mapping the Terrain of Executable Commands

Understanding where commands live and ensuring you can run them is key to mastering your Linux system.

What are Executable Commands?

- **Programs:** Think of them as tiny (or sometimes huge) tools that perform specific jobs.
- **Stand-alone:** They reside as files on your filesystem, as opposed to being built into your shell itself.
- **Need Permissions:** To run, they need the 'execute' file permission.

The Search Path

- **Your Shell's PATH:** This is an environment variable – a list of directories your shell looks in automatically when you type a command
- **Finding Your Path:** echo $PATH (Typical output looks like `/usr/local/bin:/usr/bin:/bin` – a colon-separated list)
- **Why This Matters:** Commands NOT in a PATH directory need their full location specified to run (e.g., `/home/yourname/scripts/my_cool_script`).

Scenario 1: Custom Script Woes

You made a script, `organize_photos.sh`. It works if you're *in* the directory with it, but not from anywhere else. Solution:

1. **Find a PATH directory:** echo $PATH tells you where to put it
2. **Move it:** Use `mv organize_photos.sh /usr/local/bin` (may need 'sudo' if you don't own that directory). Now just `organize_photos.sh` should work!

Scenario 2: "Command Not Found", But It Exists!

You check, the file's there, but it won't run:

1. **Permissions:** `ls -l command_name` Check if it has the 'x' (execute) permission for your user or group. If not, fix with `chmod u+x command_name` ('u+x' adds execute for the user that owns the file).

2. **Filetype:** `file command_name` Could be a script needing an interpreter (if it's a Python script, `python command_name` might be the way to run it).

Exploring Executable Locations

- **/bin and /usr/bin:** Standard commands on almost every Linux system (think 'ls', 'cp', etc.).
- **/sbin and /usr/sbin:** System administration tools, often needing 'sudo' to run.
- **/usr/local/bin:** Often where software you install manually puts its commands.
- **~/bin:** Some users make a 'bin' directory in their home for personal scripts.

Important Notes

- **Distribution Differences:** Where some executables live can vary slightly between different flavors of Linux.
- **Security:** PATH order matters! If you make a script called 'ls', and it's early in your PATH, it'll run instead of the real 'ls'! Caution with personal scripts!

Additional Resources

- **Understanding Linux File Permissions:** https://linuxize.com/post/linux-file-permissions/
- **Managing Your PATH:** https://linuxize.com/post/how-to-set-and-list-environment-variables-in-linux/

Up Next (Future Chapters)

- **Unlocking help systems (`man`, `--help`) for those executables**
- **Beyond executables: The other file types living on your Linux system**

Practice

1. **Treasure Hunt:** Pick a command from your PATH (echo $PATH to see what's there). Use the which command on it (e.g., which ls) to find its full location.
2. **Script Placement:** If you COULD add a personal directory to your PATH, where would you put it? Why?

Caution

Messing with system-critical directories in PATH can cause problems if done wrong! If unsure, experiment in a virtual machine or less important system first.

Share Your Path Discoveries

Have you stumbled upon any particularly interesting directories filled with executables on your system?

Unlocking Wisdom: Navigating Help Pages for Shell Built-Ins and Executable Commands, Part 1

Get ready to conquer the world of command-line assistance with "Unlocking Wisdom: Navigating Help Pages for Shell Built-Ins and Executable Commands, Part 1." Learn to decode the built-in documentation systems that will be your constant companions!

Why Help Pages Matter

- **Reference:** Precise option explanations, beyond what you can easily memorize.
- **Discovery:** Commands might have hidden features you never realized existed.
- **Troubleshooting:** Error messages often hint at specific options or syntax that help pages can clarify.

Help System #1: Man Pages (Manual Pages)

- **Accessing:** `man command_name` (Example: `man grep`)
- **Navigation**
    - Arrows to scroll, 'q' to quit
    - `/searchterm` (followed by Enter) to search within the page
- **Typical Man Page Structure**
    - NAME: Brief command description
    - SYNOPSIS: The 'correct' command syntax with options
    - DESCRIPTION: In-depth explanation
    - OPTIONS: Detailed breakdown of each option
    - EXAMPLES: Sometimes there to illustrate usage
    - SEE ALSO: Pointers to related commands

Scenario: Beyond Basic File Listing

You want more from 'ls' than just filenames:

1. `man ls`: Brings up the man page
2. Search for `/size` Finds options related to displaying file sizes
3. Experiment with options like `-h` (human-readable sizes)

Help System #2: The '--help' Option

- **Many (But Not All) Commands Have It:** `command_name --help` (Example: `df --help`)
- **Usually More Concise:** A quick summary, unlike the full man page
- **Great for Option Reminders:** When you know what a command does, but forget the exact switch you need.

Important Notes

- **Complexity Varies:** Some man pages are clear, others *very* technical. Don't be afraid to skip to the EXAMPLES section first for simpler commands.
- **Online Alternatives:** Many man pages are mirrored online. This can be better for searching across commands, not just within one.
- **Distro Differences:** A few commands might have slightly altered options between different Linux distributions.

Additional Resources

- **The Linux Documentation Project:** (https://www.tldp.org/): Hosts many guides and HOWTO documents, including some explaining how to read man pages effectively.

Up Next: Part 2

- **Finding help when you don't even KNOW the command name**
- **Beyond `man` and `--help`: other documentation sources**
- **What to do when help pages are still confusing**

Practice

1. **pick a common command:** Try `ls`, `cd`, or `pwd`. Look at BOTH its man page and its `--help` output. Which did you find easier to understand?
2. **Feature Hunt:** Does the 'grep' command have an option to make searches case-insensitive? Its help pages should tell you!

Pro Tip: Combining Help and Pipes

Sometimes, the output of '--help' is long. Pipe to 'less' for easier browsing!
Example: `df --help | less`

Share Your Help Discoveries

Have you ever been completely stumped by a command, and then its help page finally revealed the solution you needed?

Unlocking Wisdom: Navigating Help Pages for Shell Built-Ins and Executable Commands, Part 2

Let's go beyond the basics and tap into the full potential of Linux's hidden documentation treasures.

Scenario 1: I Don't Even Know the Command!

You need to work with .zip archives, but don't know the right tool. Help systems to the rescue!

1. **`apropos`: The Keyword Searcher**
    - `apropos zip` (Search for 'zip' in command descriptions)
    - Might get many results! Briefly describes each
2. **Targeting man: Search Within Man Pages**
    - `man -k zip` (Same as `apropos`, but outputs command names)

Scenario 2: Help Overload

You found 'tar' is for archives, but `man tar` is overwhelming. How to focus?

1. **Jump to Sections:** In 'man', try `/OPTIONS` to search directly for the options section
2. **Web Search:** For friendlier explanations, try searching "tar command examples linux" (your keywords here). Community tutorials often break things down well.

Beyond 'man' and '–help'

1. **`info` Pages:** Some commands (often GNU tools) have in-depth info pages. Try `info command_name` (Navigation is different than 'man', 'q' to quit).
2. **Command's Website:** Especially for complex software installed later, its own website might have the most structured documentation.
3. **Package Manager Docs:** If you used `apt-get` or `yum` to install something, your distro might have online docs for the package.

When Help Isn't Helping

- **Outdated Info:** Especially with less common software, documentation might lag behind the actual version you have.
- **Assumed Knowledge:** Help pages assume a certain level of Linux understanding. Don't be afraid to search for explanations of the concepts you see mentioned.
- **It's Truly Broken:** Rarely, help systems themselves have errors. This is where online communities become invaluable!

Additional Resources

- **Explainshell:** (https://explainshell.com/) Enter a command snippet, get a breakdown of each part. Great for complex command lines.

Practice

1. **Unfamiliar Territory:** Think of a task you've *never* done from the command line (Example: burning a CD). Can you use apropos to find a relevant command?
2. **The 'less' is More:** The 'less' command itself has options. Look at man less. Can you find how to make it case-insensitive for searches?

Pro Tip: Help in Scripts

Even when writing scripts, include commented lines like this for future reference:

```
# Extract specific files from a zip archive:
# See 'unzip --help' for options, especially -j
```

Share Your Discoveries

Have you ever been lost in a sea of options, only for a command's help page to illuminate the one switch you needed?

Command Compendium: Unveiling Brief Descriptions of Executable Programs

Imagine it as a field guide to the vast landscape of tools at your disposal on the Linux command line.

Why a Compendium Matters

1. **Beyond the Usual Suspects:** While you'll learn the core commands, knowing what else is out there empowers you when new problems arise.
2. **Jogging Your Memory:** Even experienced users sometimes get a "Wait, there's a command for that?" moment. A compendium is perfect for a quick refresher.
3. **Inspiration:** Sometimes just seeing what tools exist sparks ideas for automating tasks you've been doing manually!

Building Our Compendium

We'll structure our compendium with these key elements:

- **Command Name:** The obvious part!
- **One-Sentence Description:** What's its primary function?
- **Category:** (Refer to "Command Chronicles" chapters for this) File manipulation? Text processing? System info?
- **Example:** A *very basic* usage example to solidify the concept.

Compendium Snippet

Let's illustrate with a few common and some less-common commands:

Command Name	One-Sentence Description	Category	Example
df	Reports how much disk space is free on your system	System Info	df -h (for human-readable output)

grep	Searches for text patterns within files	Text Processing	`grep 'error' system.log`
gzip	Compresses files to save space	Compression	`gzip large_report .txt`
cal	Displays a calendar of the current month	System Info	`cal 9 2023` (for September 2023)
bc	An arbitrary-precision calculator (does math beyond what your shell normally handles)	Text Processing	`echo '589 * 1.06'	bc`

Challenges with a Compendium

- **Distro Differences:** Not every Linux has the *exact* same set of commands by default. This compendium is a starting point, not an absolute.
- **Depth:** One-sentence descriptions will sometimes feel inadequate. That's where man pages or further research come in once you've found the right tool's name.
- **Maintenance:** Software changes over time! A compendium is most useful if kept updated (perhaps a notes section in the chapter for readers to add their own discoveries over time).

Additional Resources

- **Cheat Sheet:** https://linuxize.com/post/linux-command-line-cheat-sheet/

Practice

1. **Your Top 10:** Not just the commands you use most, but ones you always find useful to have in your mental toolkit. Start a personal compendium!

2. **Mystery Tool:** Pick a directory in `/usr/bin`. List the files there. Can you guess what 3 of them might do just from their name? `man` will confirm!

Caution

Especially when experimenting with system-related commands you find in a compendium, be cautious if you don't fully understand them. Experiment on non-critical systems first, or within virtual machines.

Share Your 'Aha!' Moments

Have you ever stumbled upon a little-known command that completely changed how you did a certain task?

Section 5:
Crafting Custom Commands

Command Fusion: Mastering the Art of Sequential Execution, Part 1

In the world of the Linux command line, efficiency is paramount. The ability to chain commands together in a single line creates a superpower that streamlines your workflow, reduces repetition, and unlocks a whole new level of productivity. This chapter initiates your journey into the realm of command fusion. We'll focus on the sequential execution of commands; connecting the output of one command to the input of the next.

Understanding Command Pipelines: The Essence of Sequential Execution

At the heart of sequential execution lies the concept of the 'pipe' represented by the vertical bar character (|). The pipe takes the output (standard output) of the command on its left and seamlessly redirects it as input (standard input) to the command on its right. Think of it as a series of interconnected waterways. Here's a simple example:

```
ls -l | less
```

In this example:

1. `ls -l` generates a long directory listing
2. The pipe (|) takes that listing output
3. The `less` command receives it, allowing you to scroll through the listing conveniently

The Power of Combining Commands

Let's illustrate with a few more scenarios to highlight the potential of command fusion:

- **Filtering Results:** Want to find files ending with ".txt" in a directory?

```
ls | grep ".txt"
```

Here, `grep` filters the output of `ls`

- **Counting Items:** Need to quickly count the number of files in your home directory?

```
ls ~ | wc -l
```

The `wc -l` command counts the lines fed to it (which correspond to files).

Complex Transformations: Let's say you want a list of unique IP addresses from your web server's log file sorted in reverse order:

```
cat /var/log/apache2/access.log | awk '{ print $1 }' |
sort | uniq | sort -r
```

- This chain might seem intimidating at first, but it works beautifully:
  - `cat` reads the log file
  - `awk` extracts the first field (IP address)
  - `sort` puts them in order
  - `uniq` removes duplicates
  - `sort -r` gives a reverse-sorted list

Important Considerations

Before we dive deeper, keep in mind:

- **Success and Error:** In a pipeline, generally, the success of one command is needed for the next one to work. If a command fails, the pipeline usually stops.
- **Standard Output vs. Standard Error:** Pipes primarily work with standard output. Error messages (standard error) are still printed to the terminal unless redirected (we'll cover this later).

Harnessing Operators: Redirecting Output and Error

Sometimes you might want to send the output of a command to a file or handle error messages differently. Here are some key operators:

- **> (Redirection):** Sends standard output to a file. For example:

```
ls -l > directory_listing.txt
```

- **>> (Appending):** Appends standard output to a file (instead of overwriting):

```
find / -name "*.log" >> log_locations.txt
```

- **2> (Error Redirection):** Redirects the error output (standard error) to a file:

```
some_command 2> errors.txt
```

Mastering Sequential Execution: Best Practices

1. **Start Small, Build Complexity:** Begin with simple commands, gradually adding more as you get comfortable.
2. **Test Thoroughly:** Experiment with different pipelines to ensure they function as expected.
3. **Debug Smartly:** If a pipeline fails, break it into smaller chunks to isolate the problem point.
4. **Embrace Creativity:** The more you practice, the more creative solutions you'll discover.

Additional Resources

- **Linux Documentation Project - The Power of Pipelines and Redirection:** https://tldp.org/LDP/abs/html/io-redirection.html
- **ExplainShell - Understand Your Commands:** https://explainshell.com/

Part 2 Preview

In the next part, we'll delve into controlling execution flow with logical operators, making your command fusion techniques even more powerful!

Command Fusion: Mastering the Art of Sequential Execution, Part 2

In the previous chapter, we began our command fusion journey with pipes (|). These form the backbone for linearly chaining commands, connecting the output of one to the input of the next. In this chapter, we'll upgrade our toolkit with logical operators, empowering us to control how commands work together, giving you even more command-line mastery.

The Power of Logical Operators

Let's introduce three essential logical operators:

- **&& (AND):** This operator executes the second command *only if* the first command succeeds (gives an exit status of zero).
  Example:

```
mkdir new_directory && cd new_directory
```

  Here, you'll change into your newly created directory (new_directory) only if its creation was successful.

- **|| (OR):** This operator executes the second command *only if* the first command fails (gives a non-zero exit status).
  Example:

```
rm some_file.txt || echo "File not found!"
```

  This command attempts to remove some_file.txt, and if it doesn't exist, it neatly prints a message.

- **; (Semicolon):** A simple but essential operator, the semicolon allows you to execute multiple commands in sequence, regardless of whether the previous commands succeed or fail.

  Example:

```
ls -l; date; pwd
```

  This chain will perform a directory listing, display the current date, and then show your present working directory.

Combining Operators for Complex Logic

The magic begins when you strategically combine these operators:

- **Conditional File Creation:** Let's say you only want to create a file if it doesn't exist:

```
test -f important_data.txt || touch important_data.txt
```

Here, `test -f` checks if the file exists. If it doesn't, the second command with `touch` runs.

- **Cleanup with Caution:** Want to delete a temporary file, but only if it was successfully modified?

```
nano temp_workfile.txt && rm temp_workfile.txt
```

With &&, the file removal happens only if you've edited and saved within nano.

- **Handling Possibilities:** Sometimes you may have multiple success states:

```
ping -c 1 google.com || ping -c 1 cloudflare.com ||
echo "No internet connection!"
```

This attempts to ping two reliable hosts. If either responds, you know you're online. If both fail, you get an error message.

Controlling Execution Flow: Best Practices

1. **Break Down Problems:** When complex logic is needed, break the task into smaller, manageable commands connected with logical operators.
2. **Test, Then Test Again:** A few mismatched operators can lead to unexpected results. Test your command chains rigorously.
3. **Error Handling:** Consider using || to trigger alternative actions if a critical part of your chain fails, helping you avoid surprises.
4. **Readability Counts:** While it's tempting to cram everything in one line, consider using semicolons or line breaks for longer chains for the sake of your future self and anyone else deciphering your work.

Additional Resources

- **Linux Shell Scripting Tutorial (v2.0) - Logical Operators:**
  https://ryanstutorials.net/bash-scripting-tutorial/bash-logical-operators.php
- **The Bash Hackers Wiki - Logical Operators:**
  http://wiki.bash-hackers.org/commands/classictest#logical_combinations

Key Takeaways

- Logical operators (&&, | |, ;) give you precise control over command execution flow.
- Use them strategically to handle success/failure cases and chain commands in creative ways.

Coming Up Next

We've only scratched the surface of command fusion! Get ready to unleash your inner wildcard wizard. In the next chapter, we'll explore how wildcards expand your ability to work with multiple files and directories at lightning speed.

Unleashing the Wild: Harnessing Powerful Wildcards for Command Mastery, Part 1

In the Linux command line, efficiency is paramount. Wildcards are special characters that function as flexible placeholders, letting you specify groups of files or directories that match a certain pattern. Mastering the use of wildcards makes repetitive tasks lightning fast and reduces the chances of typos. Imagine being able to delete old log files, or copy specific types of documents from multiple locations in a single command!

The Basics: Meet the Wildcards

Let's introduce the two most important wildcards:

- **The Asterisk (*)** This powerful symbol represents **zero or more** characters. Let's see some examples:
    - `report*.txt`: Matches "report.txt", "report_final.txt", "report2023_Jan.txt", etc.
    - `data*.csv`: Matches "data.csv", "data_backup.csv", "data_old_1203.csv", etc.
    - `temp*`: Matches any file or directory starting with "temp"
- **The Question Mark (?)** This wildcard represents a **single** character.
    - `data_??.log`: Matches "data_01.log", "data_AB.log", but not "data_123.log".
    - `backup_2023??15.zip`: Matches "backup_20230315.zip", "backup_20231215.zip", etc.

Wildcards in Action

Let's see how wildcards bring efficiency to common command-line tasks:

1. **Selective File Removal:** You want to delete all PDF files from a directory filled with other important files. Here's the command:

```
rm *.pdf
```

2. **File Renaming in Bulk:** Imagine renaming a series of files like "image1.jpg", "image2.jpg" to "trip1.jpg", "trip2.jpg", etc. Wildcards to the rescue:

```
mv image?.jpg trip?.jpg
```

3. **Copying Specific File Types:** Want to copy all the markdown files starting with "chapter" from multiple sub-directories into your current directory?

```
cp */chapter*.md .
```

Combining Wildcards for Extra Power

You can strategically combine wildcards to craft sophisticated matching patterns.

- **Matching Text within Filenames:** Let's say you want to list all files containing the word "draft" anywhere in the filename:

```
ls *draft*
```

- **Targeting File Extensions:** Need to find all backup files, which could have .bak, .backup, or related extensions?

```
find . -name "*.bak*"
```

Tips and Cautions

- **Hidden Files:** Remember, wildcards like * by default don't match hidden files (filenames starting with a dot). To include them, you might need to modify patterns (e.g., .* for any file, including hidden) or use specific options with your commands.
- **Unexpected Expansion:** Use the ls command first to test the effects of your wildcards before using them with destructive commands like rm.
- **Quoting:** In scenarios with complex filenames, it may be necessary to quote your pattern (e.g., rm 'Invoices*.pdf') to prevent the shell from misinterpreting them before the command executes.

Additional Resources

- **Regular Expressions Tutorial** (https://www.regular-expressions.info/):
  While we're just scratching the surface, regular expressions are a
  broader language that uses patterns for sophisticated text matching
  (way beyond basic wildcards).
- **explainshell.com** (https://explainshell.com/): A fantastic resource for
  breaking down the actions of commands using wildcards and other
  components.

Part 2 Preview

The fun is just beginning! In the next part, we'll dive deeper into wildcards,
exploring how to filter results, exclude patterns, and unleash their full potential
to streamline your workflow.

Unleashing the Wild: Harnessing Powerful Wildcards for Command Mastery, Part 2

Controlling Wildcard Behavior with Character Classes

In Part 1, we introduced the fundamentals of the asterisk (*) and the question mark (?). Now, let's unlock more precision using character classes:

- **Character Classes** are defined within square brackets ([ ]). They match a single character, but only if it appears within the specified set or range. Here's how they work:
  - `report[0-9].txt`: Matches "report1.txt", "report2.txt", etc. (any single digit).
  - `file[a-d]`: Matches "filea", "fileb", "filec", and "filed" (lowercase a through d).
  - `image[XY]`: Matches only "imageX" or "imageY".

Negating Matches: The Power of Exclusion

Sometimes, you need to specify what you *don't* want to match. Here's how we achieve this:

- **The Exclamation Mark (!)** placed within character classes negates the character class.
  - `image[!0-9].jpg`: Matches image files that don't contain a number in the filename (useful if you have image1.jpg, image2.jpg, but also image_temp.jpg that you want to exclude).

Common Character Class Shortcuts

There are convenient shortcuts for frequently used character classes. Let's look at some:

- **[:digit:]**: Equivalent to [0-9], matching numeric digits.
- **[:alpha:]**: Equivalent to [a-zA-Z], matching alphabetical characters.
- **[:alnum:]**: Combines the above, matching letters and numbers.
- **[:space:]**: Matches whitespace characters (spaces, tabs, etc.).

Examples of Character Classes in Action

1. **Filtering Specific File Extensions:** Let's say you want to find code files but need to include various extensions

   ```
   find . -name "*.[chj]pp"
   ```

2. **Targeting Date-based Backups:** Imagine you have backups named "backup_20230314.tar.gz", "backup_20230315.tar.gz" and so on:

   ```
   ls backup_2023[0-9][0-9][0-1][0-9].tar.gz
   ```

   This ensures you match two-digit months and two-digit days.

Wildcards in Advanced Command Combinations

Let's see how wildcards empower even more complex actions:

- **Finding and Executing:** Ever needed to find files of a specific type and perform an operation on them? The `find` command paired with `-exec` is your friend:

  ```
  find . -name '*.bak' -exec rm -i {} \;
  ```

  This finds backup files (ending with .bak), and executes `rm -i` for each one (the `-i` prompts before deletion). Remember, the `{} \;` is the magic part!

- **Complex File Copies:** Need to copy all text (.txt) and markdown (.md) files, excluding drafts, from various directories into a central "archive" folder?

  ```
  mkdir archive
   cp */[!drafts]*.{txt,md} archive/
  ```

Cautions and Best Practices

- **Test with Care:** Always test wildcard-based commands with `ls` or `echo` before using them with destructive actions like `rm`. A small typo can have big consequences!

- **Specificity is Key:** The more specific your wildcards, the less likely you'll have unintended matches.
- **When in Doubt, Quote:** It's sometimes safer, especially with complex filenames, to quote your wildcard pattern: `cp 'Photo Album*.jpg' destination/`. This prevents the shell from misinterpreting the pattern before the command runs.

Additional Resources

- **The Bash Reference Manual - Pattern Matching:** https://www.gnu.org/software/bash/manual/html_node/Pattern-Matching.html
- **Linux Documentation Project - Using Wildcard Characters and Ranges:** https://tldp.org/LDP/abs/html/globbingref.html]

The Wild World of Commands Awaits

Wildcards transform your command line efficiency. Embrace experimentation, practice, and before long these powerful patterns will become an intuitive part of your workflow!

Delving Deeper into Wildcard Wonders, Part 1

Harnessing wildcards unlocks incredible flexibility on the command line, but their true power lies in the intricate ways they interact with other commands and operators. In this chapter, we'll venture further into this realm, helping you see wildcards not just as simple matching tools, but as building blocks for sophisticated file management.

The Brace Expansion: Generating Alternatives

Sometimes, you need to execute the same command with minor variations. Brace expansion provides an elegant way to streamline this process:

- **Syntax:** {option1,option2,option3...}
- **Example 1:** Want to create multiple directories quickly?

```
mkdir project_{backup,data,docs}
```

This is equivalent to running `mkdir project_backup mkdir project_data`, `mkdir project_docs`.

- **Example 2:** Compressing files with different extensions:

```
gzip report.{txt,csv,log}
```

Combining Brace Expansion with Wildcards

Brace expansion and wildcards become a dynamic duo when used together:

- **Handling Variations:** Need to move files having slight naming inconsistencies?

```
mv old_report_{final,latest}.txt reports/
```

This covers "old_report_final.txt", "old_report_latest.txt", etc.

- **Targeting Multiple Directories:** Performing operations across multiple directories:

```
find Documents/{Vacation1,Vacation2,Work} -name
'*.jpg'
```

Looks for JPEG images in the specified Vacation and Work subdirectories.

Controlling Brace Expansion's Behavior

Let's uncover a few tricks to customize how brace expansions work.

- **Nested Braces:** Create more complex variations.

```
touch file{1,2}_{old,new}.txt
```

This results in files like file1_old.txt, file1_new.txt, file2_old.txt, file2_new.txt.

- **Disabling Brace Expansion:** Sometimes, you want the literal braces. Escape them with a backslash (\):

```
echo \{option1,option2\}   # This will print
{option1,option2}
```

Advanced File Manipulation Strategies

Let's apply our skills to some real-world scenarios with wildcards and brace expansion at their core:

1. **Selective Batch Editing:** Imagine you have image files named "img_001.jpg", "img_002.jpg" and similarly for PNGs, and want to resize them all. Try this:

```
mkdir resized
mogrify -resize 50% *.{jpg,png} -path resized/
```

The `mogrify` command resizes with wildcards, the brace expansion handles the different extensions.

2. **Cleanup with Precision:** You've downloaded several versions of a large file "project_data_v1.zip", "project_data_v2.zip", and so on. Cleaning up selectively:

```
rm project_data_v{1,2,3}.zip  # Keeps the latest
versions intact
```

Word of Caution

Brace expansion happens *before* wildcard expansion by the shell. If you have many possible expansions, this can overload your command line with too many arguments. Test first!

Additional Resources

- **A Deeper Look at Bash Brace Expansion:**
  https://www.gnu.org/software/bash/manual/html_node/Brace-Expansion.html

Part 2: More Expansions and Loops

In the next chapter, we'll introduce range expansions within braces, and how combining wildcards with loops opens a whole new territory for automating complex command-line tasks.

Experiment and Refine

The best way to master wildcards and brace expansions is to practice. Start with small examples, gradually increasing complexity, and refer to the resources for guidance.

Delving Deeper into Wildcard Wonders, Part 2

Range Expansions: Number Sequences and More

The brace expansion technique we saw earlier can streamline more than just comma-separated values. Let's introduce range expansions:

- **Numbers:** echo {1..10} will print numbers from 1 to 10. You can specify increments, like echo {1..10..2} (1, 3, 5, 7, 9).
- **Letters:** echo {A..E} prints capital letters A to E. For both numbers and letters, ranges must be in sequential order.

Examples of Range Expansions in Practice

1. **Quick File Creation:** Want to create multiple empty files at once?

```
touch report_{01..05}.txt
```

2. **Downloading Sequences:** Need to grab images from a web server with sequential numbering?

```
wget https://images.com/image_{001..100}.jpg
```

Combining Expansions: The Power of Nesting

Remember, you can nest different types of expansions for versatile combinations:

```
echo section_{A..C}_{1..3}.pdf
```

This generates filenames section_A_1.pdf, section_A_2.pdf... section_C_3.pdf, and so on. Get creative!

Wildcards and Loops: A Dynamic Duo

Loops in shell scripting are a powerful way to iterate commands. Wildcards make them even more flexible for file operations. Here's the basic structure of a 'for loop':

```
for item in some_list;
```

```
 do
    commands_to_run_on_item
done
```

Let's see it in action:

- **Renaming with Numbers:** Say you have a bunch of image files you want to add a sequence number to:

```
counter=1
for image in *.jpg;
 do
    mv "$image" "landscape_$counter.jpg"
    counter=$((counter+1))
done
```

- **Searching within Specific Files:** Need to search for a phrase within all Python scripts in a directory?

```
for script in *.py;
 do
    grep 'search_term' "$script"
 done
```

Things to Consider with Loops

- **Handling Spaces in Filenames:** When iterating over files, always quote your variables (e.g., "$item") to prevent issues with spaces.
- **Testing Before Bulk Actions:** If performing destructive operations like renaming or deleting, do a test run with echo to see what the loop will do before executing the real commands.

Additional Resources:

- **Shell Scripting Tutorial - for Loop**
  https://www.shellscript.sh/loops.html
- **Wikipedia - Glob (programming)**
  (https://en.wikipedia.org/wiki/Glob_(programming))

Advanced Loop Techniques (Teaser)

In more complex scenarios, you might combine `find` with the `-exec` option and use wildcards within your loop commands. We'll delve into these powerful techniques in a future chapter!

Tips for Mastering Expansions and Loops

1. **Start Small, Scale Up:** Begin with simple brace expansions and loops to get the basic form down. Then, gradually add complexity.
2. **Quote Liberally:** Use quotes around variables and expansions, particularly spaces are involved, to avoid unintended behavior.
3. **Test, Test, Test!** Always test commands before executing them with destructive options.

Let's Automate!

Think of tasks you repeat frequently on the command line, especially ones involving groups of files. Are there any that could be automated by cleverly combining wildcards, expansions, and loops?

Command Customization: Crafting Personalized Linux Commands with the alias Feature, Part 1

The terminal is your command center in Linux. One incredible way to personalize this experience is by utilizing the 'alias' feature. Think of aliases as custom shortcuts or powerful abbreviations for the commands you use most. With them, you can simplify complex commands, streamline your workflow, and overcome those pesky typos!

The Anatomy of an Alias

Here's the basic structure of a simple alias declaration:

```
alias short_name='longer_command_or_commands'
```

Let's break it down:

- **alias:** The keyword that tells the shell you're creating an alias.
- **short_name:** Your chosen shortcut. Be descriptive and memorable.
- **'longer_command_or_commands':** The actual command (or series of commands) you want to represent. Crucially, this part is enclosed within quotes to ensure the shell interprets it correctly.

Alias in Action: Examples

1. **Abbreviating Lengthy Commands:**

```
alias update='sudo apt update && sudo apt upgrade'
```

Now, instead of typing that whole sequence, you simply type update.

2. **Fixing Common Typos:**

```
alias gerp='grep'
```

No more mistyping one of the most common search commands!

3. **Adding Default Options:**

```
alias ls='ls --color=auto -l'
```

Now every `ls` command uses colors for easy distinction of file types and displays detailed file information.

Making Aliases Available: Shells and Sessions

- **Current Session:** When you define an alias directly in your terminal, it exists only within the current session. Close your terminal, and it's gone.
- **Persistence:** To make aliases permanent, you need to save them in your shell's configuration files. These usually include:
  - `~/.bashrc` (for the Bash shell)
  - `~/.zshrc` (for the Zsh shell)

Editing Configuration Files

1. Use your favorite text editor (e.g., `nano ~/.bashrc`)
2. Add your alias definitions, one per line, at the end of the file.
3. Save the changes.
4. Source the modified file to apply changes in the current session: `. ~/.bashrc` or `. ~/.zshrc`

Viewing Your Aliases

To view a list of currently active aliases in your session, simply type:

```
alias
```

Tips for Crafting Effective Aliases

1. **Keep It Short and Sweet:** The whole point is to save keystrokes.
2. **Be Descriptive:** The alias name should hint at its function.
3. **Avoid Overriding Existing Commands:** Check if your alias name conflicts with an existing command to prevent unexpected behavior.
4. **Test Before Saving:** Define your alias in your terminal first to ensure it works as intended before making it permanent.

Additional Resources

- **Linux Handbook - Aliases** https://linuxhandbook.com/linux-aliases/
- **HowToGeek: Create Aliases on Linux** https://www.howtogeek.com/73768/how-to-use-aliases-to-customize-ubuntu-commands/

Part 2 Sneak Peek

In the next part, we'll dive into more sophisticated aliases - passing arguments, combining aliases within other commands, and the power of shell functions for even more complex customizations.

Your Custom Workflow

Think about commands you use frequently, long commands with options, or places where you have stubborn typos. Could you streamline these with aliases?

Unveiling the Power of Aliases: Expanding Command Potential, Part 2

Passing Arguments: When Aliases Get Dynamic

In Part 1, we covered simple aliases. But their true power is unleashed when you make them accept arguments. Let's see how:

- **Placeholders:** Within your alias, use numbered placeholders like $1, $2, $3 etc., to represent arguments passed to your alias.

Examples

1. **Searching Within Specific Directories:**

```
alias search='find $1 -name "*$2*"'
```

   Now you can: `search /home/john report` to find files containing "report" within John's home directory.

2. **Compressing with Choices:**

```
alias zipit='gzip -9 $1'  # For maximum compression
alias zipfast='gzip -1 $1'  # For faster compression
```

Handling Complex Arguments

For arguments with spaces or special characters, use double quotes around your placeholders to treat them as a single unit:

```
alias mvsafe='mv "$1" ~/backup_dir/"$1"'
```

This prevents issues if you run: `mvsafe "My Project Report.txt"`

Unleashing Your Custom Toolkit

Think of common tasks that involve a base command but have variations in directories, filenames, or options. Aliases with arguments are your solution!

Aliases within Aliases - Caution!

While you *can* technically use aliases within other aliases, proceed with caution. Recursive aliases (an alias used inside its own definition) can lead to unexpected behavior or infinite loops. It's generally safer to expand aliases manually if nesting is necessary.

When Aliases Aren't Enough: Shell Functions

Let's introduce the idea of shell functions for situations where you need more than simple command substitutions:

```
function complex_process () {
   command1  # Can have multiple commands
   if [ condition ]; then  # Conditional logic allowed
      command2
   else
      command3
   fi
}
```

- **Key Differences from Aliases:**
    - Aliases are primarily for substituting commands and simplifying syntax.
    - Shell functions allow for more complex scripting with control flow logic (if-statements, loops, etc.) directly within your terminal session.

Choosing the Right Tool

- **Quick Shortcuts & Options:** Aliases are perfect.
- **Conditional Actions or Multiple Commands:** Consider shell functions.

Tips for Mastering Aliases with Arguments:

- **Test Thoroughly:** Use echo to preview the expanded alias before execution with complex arguments.
- **Double-Check Quoting:** Ensure arguments containing spaces or special characters are correctly quoted within your alias definitions.
- **Organize Your Configuration:** In your .bashrc or .zshrc, keep aliases well-structured and optionally commented for future you!

Additional Resources:

- **How-To Geek: How to Create Your Own Shell Functions on Linux**
  https://www.howtogeek.com/287350/how-to-create-your-own-shell-functions-on-linux/

Part 3: The Cleanup Crew

In our final installment, we'll learn how to delete aliases you no longer use, strategize saving your best customizations, and consider long-term organization for your command-line productivity toolbox.

What are some multi-step or complex command combinations you'd like to turn into aliases?

Managing Aliases: Deleting and Saving Customizations for Long-Term Efficiency, Part 3

Housekeeping for Your Aliases

As your alias collection grows, you might find:

- **Outdated Shortcuts:** Some aliases may no longer be relevant to your workflow.
- **Naming Conflicts:** New aliases could clash with existing commands or with each other.
- **Temporary Tweaks:** You create some aliases on the fly and forget about them.

Let's clean up and solidify your best ones!

Step 1: Review Your Current Aliases

Start by listing what you have:

```
alias
```

Step 2: Remove the Unnecessary

Use the `unalias` command to delete aliases you don't need anymore:

```
unalias old_shortcut
unalias another_one
```

- **Important:** Changes made with `unalias` are for your current session only. We'll make them permanent next.

Step 3: Editing Configuration Files

1. Open your shell configuration file (`~/.bashrc` for Bash, `~/.zshrc` for Zsh) in your preferred text editor.
2. Locate any aliases you want to remove and delete the lines containing them.
3. Save the changes.

Step 4: Apply Changes

Source your configuration file to make these updates active in your current terminal session:

```
source ~/.bashrc    # Or source ~/.zshrc if you use Zsh
```

Best Practices for Organizing Aliases

1. **Dedicated Alias File:** Consider creating a separate file (e.g., `~/.aliases`) specifically for your aliases. Then, in your `.bashrc` or `.zshrc`:

```
source ~/.aliases
```

2. **Comments:** Add comments above your alias definitions to explain their function, especially for complex ones. Future you will be thankful!

```
# Updates system and upgrades packages
alias update='sudo apt update && sudo apt upgrade'
```

3. **Version Control (Advanced):** If you're tech-savvy, use a version control system like Git to track your alias files. This allows you to easily revert to previous configurations and collaborate with others.

When Aliases Might Not Be the Ideal Solution

- **Complex Logic:** When you need intricate conditional actions or looping, shell functions are a better fit. Think of them as 'mini-scripts' within your shell.
- **Shared Customizations:** If multiple users on a system should benefit from aliases or functions, consider placing them in a system-wide configuration file (be cautious with permissions in this case).

Additional Resources

- **How Do I Create a Permanent Bash Alias - Ask Ubuntu**
  https://askubuntu.com/questions/17536/how-do-i-create-a-permanent-bash-alias

Beyond Aliases: The Journey Continues

The command-line is about making the environment work for *you*. Your aliases are now a well-maintained tool in your arsenal. But don't stop there! Explore shell functions, scripting, and the vast ecosystem of command-line utilities to mold Linux into your ultimate productivity machine.

Let's Reflect

- Were there any aliases you decided to remove during the cleanup?
- Do you have any existing shell functions? Could you streamline some of them, or would certain tasks be better as new aliases?

Section 6:
Advanced Command–Line Techniques

Performance Tuning: Optimizing Your System for Speed and Efficiency

Understanding Bottlenecks: Where Things Slow Down

Before blindly applying fixes, it's wise to understand the *source* of slowness. Often, the culprits are:

- **Resource Exhaustion:** Your system runs out of available RAM, CPU power, or disk space.
- **Disk I/O:** Slow hard drives (especially mechanical ones) bottleneck the system if data access is the limiting factor.
- **Network Issues:** A slow internet connection or network problems can make everything feel sluggish.
- **Unnecessary Services/Programs:** Background processes consuming resources you need elsewhere.
- **Misconfiguration:** Software settings may be unintentionally hampering performance.

The Toolkit: Commands for Investigation

1. ****top **** or **htop**: These give you a real-time overview of processes, CPU usage, memory usage, and more. Look for processes hogging resources. (htop is similar to top but often considered more user-friendly)
2. **free -m**: Displays available and used memory (RAM) in megabytes.
3. **df -h**: Shows disk space usage for mounted filesystems in human-readable format.
4. **vmstat**: Provides information about processes, memory, I/O, CPU activity, and more. Look out for high numbers in the 'block' I/O columns (bi, bo) as these suggest a slow disk.
5. **iostat**: Specifically monitors storage device (disks) input/output statistics.

Optimization Tactics

Let's explore strategies targeting the common bottlenecks:

Strategy 1: Freeing Up Resources

- **Kill Unnecessary Processes:** Identify greedy processes with `top` or `htop`. Use `kill process_ID` or `killall process_name` (use these cautiously).
- **Manage Startup Applications:** Many GUI distros have built-in tools. Command-line way: investigate `~/.config/autostart` or system-level startup scripts (varies by distribution).
- **Change Desktop Environment:** Lighter-weight desktops (XFCE, LXDE) use less RAM, ideal for older machines.

Strategy 2: Disk Optimization Techniques

- **Upgrade to an SSD:** One of the *best* performance upgrades if you're still using a mechanical hard drive (HDD).
- **I/O scheduler:** `cat /sys/block/sda/queue/scheduler` (replace 'sda' with your drive name) may reveal a changeable setting. Tweaking this is more advanced (research before changing).
- **Clean Up Disk Space:** Delete unnecessary files, or use a tool like `bleachbit`

Strategy 3: Reduce Network Latency

- **Test Connection:** `ping` to servers or your router will measure network latency.
- **DNS Check:** A faster DNS server may improve speeds (`nmcli dev show` reveals your current settings).
- **Background Network Usage:** Monitor with tools like `nethogs` to identify applications consuming bandwidth you need.

Strategy 4: General Performance Tuning

- **Services Audit:** `systemctl list-unit-files –type=service` shows services. Disable unneeded ones (`systemctl disable service_name` – be cautious, research if unsure!).
- **System Updates:** `sudo apt update && sudo apt upgrade` (or your distro's equivalent) might fix performance bugs.

- **Kernel Parameters:** Tweaking kernel settings is very advanced, but tools like 'tuned' can offer pre-built profiles for different workloads.

Important Considerations

- **Backups First:** Always create backups or system snapshots before major changes, just in case!
- **Gradual Change:** Apply optimizations one at a time, retesting performance to evaluate the effect.
- **Don't Over-Optimize:** Perfect is the enemy of good. At some point, further gains become minuscule.

Additional Resources:

- **How To Use the Linux top Command**
  https://linuxize.com/post/linux-top-command/
- **The Ultimate Guide to Linux System Monitoring Tools**
  https://linuxhandbook.com/linux-system-monitoring-tools/

This is Just the Beginning

Performance tuning is an ongoing exploration. The command line grants you insights and control!

Advanced Command-Line Utilities: Harnessing Powerful Tools for Productivity

Caution: While many of these tools come standard with popular Linux distributions, some might require installation. Check your distribution's package manager (`apt`, `dnf`, etc.)

Category 1: File Management & Manipulation

1. **rsync:** The Swiss army knife of file synchronization and copying. Ideal for backups, mirroring data across locations, and efficient large file transfers.
   - **Example:** `rsync -avz /home/john/ project_data remote_server:/backups/` (recursive, detailed, compressed transfer)
2. **find (and Advanced Usage):** While we've introduced its basics, `find` hides incredible power for complex searches:
   - **By File Type:** `find /path/ -type f -name '*.pdf'`
   - **By Size:** `find /path/ -size +1G` (files larger than 1 gigabyte)
   - **By Modification Time:** `find /path -mtime -7` (modified within the last 7 days)
   - **Actions:** `find /path/ -mtime +30 -exec rm -f {} \;` (delete files over 30 days old!)
3. **shred:** Goes beyond `rm` for secure deletion. It repeatedly overwrites file data making recovery nearly impossible.
   - **Example:** `shred -uvz -n 20 secret_file.txt` (verbose, overwrite 20 times, then zero out)

Category 2: Text Processing Powerhouses

1. **grep:** You know its basic filtering, but let's go further:
   - **Recursion:** `grep -r "search_term" /path/` (searches all files within a directory tree)
   - **Inverse Matches:** `grep -v "pattern" file.txt` (shows lines *not* matching)

- **Regular Expressions:** A whole other topic, but unlocks complex pattern matching within grep
2. **sed:** A stream editor for in-place file modification. Think of it as programmatic search and replace.
    - **Basic Substitution:** `sed 's/old_text/new_text/g file.txt > new_file.txt`
3. **awk:** A mini-programming language for text manipulation. When simple isn't enough.
    - **Example:** `awk '{print $2 "," $NF}' data.txt` (prints the second and last column of each line)

Category 3: System Monitoring & Analysis

1. **strace:** Traces system calls made by a process. Invaluable for debugging and understanding what a program does behind the scenes.
2. **ltrace:** Similar to `strace`, but tracks library calls made by a process.
3. **sar** and **sysstat** : Collect and report various system performance metrics (CPU, memory, I/O). Use for historical trends and bottleneck identification.

Category 4: Networking Swiss Army Knives

1. **nmap:** The network mapper. Scans networks, identifies active hosts, open ports, and even attempts to fingerprint operating systems.
    - **Example:** `nmap -sS -Pn 192.168.1.0/24` (Stealthy SYN scan, no ping, on the local network)
2. **netcat (nc):** Raw network connections. Used for transferring data, creating makeshift servers, or port testing. Incredibly versatile.
3. **curl:** Swiss army knife for data transfers. Supports a plethora of protocols like HTTP, FTP, SCP, and more.
    - **Example**: `curl -O https://example.com/big_download.zip`

Category 5: Miscellaneous Awesomeness

1. **tmux (or screen):** Terminal multiplexers allow multiple sessions within a single terminal window. Detach, reattach – perfect for long-running tasks.
2. **htop:** We mentioned it earlier, but consider it the interactive upgrade to `top`.

3. **imagemagick:** Command-line image manipulation wizardry (convert, resize, add effects).

This is Just a Taste

The world of command-line utilities is vast! Here's how to find even more:

- **Your Distribution's Package Manager:** Explore beyond the defaults.
- **Dedicated Repos:** Projects like awesome-cli-apps: https://github.com/agarrharr/awesome-cli-apps curate amazing tools.
- **Distro-Specific Tools:** Many distros have their own power utilities.

Important Reminders

- **Man Pages are Your Friend:** The ultimate reference. `man tool_name`
- **Caution with Online Examples:** Understand commands before running them, especially those piped to a shell!
- **Test Before Deploying:** When scripting with advanced tools, test in safe environments.

Let's Boost Your Workflow

- Do you have tasks with repetitive file manipulation steps? Maybe awk or sed could streamline them!
- Are you curious about what a program is *really* doing under the hood? strace or ltrace might be the answer.

System Monitoring: Keeping a Pulse on System Health and Performance

In this chapter, we'll dive into the art of Linux system monitoring from the command line. Think of it as putting a stethoscope to your computer to ensure it's running in tip-top shape and to spot potential problems before they become critical.

Why Monitoring Matters

Command-line system monitoring provides:

- **Real-Time Insights:** See the state of your system *right now*.
- **Resource Usage Visibility:** Understand how heavily CPU, memory, and disk I/O are being used.
- **Bottleneck Identification:** See what's slowing down your system.
- **Proactive Problem Solving:** Catch issues early, preventing downtime.
- **Trend Analysis (Longitudinal):** Tools that log data over time help spot gradual degradation in performance.

Core Areas to Monitor

1. **CPU Utilization:** The heart of your system. Is it overworked, or are there unused cores?
2. **Memory (RAM) Usage:** Does your system have enough breathing room, or is it constantly scrambling for memory (swapping)?
3. **Disk I/O:** How quickly data is read from and written to disks. Bottlenecks here cripple system responsiveness.
4. **Network Activity:** Monitoring bandwidth usage, traffic types, and connection issues are crucial for networked systems
5. **Process Health:** Keeping an eye on what programs are running, their resource consumption, and spotting any potential troublemakers.

Our Toolkit: Essential Commands

Let's revisit some familiar tools with a monitoring focus, and introduce some new ones:

- **top (or htop):** The classic, real-time overview of processes, CPU, and memory. Focus on the %CPU column, 'Mem' section, and individual process sorting.

- **free:** Memory snapshot. Look at 'free' and 'available' under the Mem row. Swap usage is a red flag.
- **df:** Disk usage per partition. Look for nearly full filesystems.
- **iostat:** Detailed disk input/output statistics. High wait times (await) suggest an overworked disk.
- **vmstat:** Provides a broader view of system state (memory, I/O, CPU, even context switching – advanced)
- **netstat:** Network status. Useful variations include `netstat -s` (summary by protocol), `netstat -i` (interface stats), `netstat -r` (routing table).
- **sar (sysstat):** Versatile collector. Can be configured to record historical performance data.

Continuous Monitoring

For ongoing monitoring, consider these tools:

- **glances:** Like an enhanced 'top', presented beautifully.
- **nmon:** Visual system monitor. Interactive mode allows switching between resources like CPU, disk, network, etc.
- **System Logging:** Services like `rsyslog` or `journalctl` are your long-term record. Filtering logs helps investigate specific events.

Interpreting the Data

Monitoring is as much about interpretation as it is about the tools themselves:

- **Spikes vs. Sustained Load:** Is a CPU spike temporary, or is your system consistently struggling?
- **Memory Leaks:** Does a process slowly consume more RAM over time, suggesting a bug?
- **Unexpected Disk Activity:** Is a program heavily churning on the disk when it shouldn't be?
- **Baselines:** Understanding what's "normal" for *your* system is crucial to detect anomalies.

Additional Resources

- **Linux Monitoring Tools: A Comprehensive guide**
  https://www.tecmint.com/top-best-linux-monitoring-tools/
- **The Ultimate Guide to Linux System Monitoring Tools**
  https://linuxhandbook.com/linux-system-monitoring-tools/

When to Go Deeper

For complex issues or specialized servers, explore:

- **Specialized Monitoring Tools:** Databases, web servers, etc., may have dedicated monitoring commands or protocols.
- **Monitoring Systems:** Nagios, Zabbix, etc., are robust solutions for large-scale monitoring, alerting, and historical data.
- **Profiling** Tools like `perf` delve into performance analysis at the code level (very advanced)

Proactive Monitoring: A Best Practice

Don't wait for failure!

- **Set Up Alerts:** Some tools can be configured with basic alerts (e.g., email when disk space is low).
- **Log Analysis:** Schedule time to review logs, spot emerging trends, and pre-empt problems.

Monitoring Challenge!

Let's simulate some scenarios:

1. **High CPU Usage:** Run `yes > /dev/null &` (forks a process doing nothing, consuming CPU). Observe in `top`. How do you terminate it? ([Let me know if you'd like an explanation of this sneaky command])
2. **RAM depletion:** Tools like `stress` can allocate memory for testing. Observe the effect on 'available' memory using `free -m`.

Networking Mastery: Enhancing Connectivity and Communication with Command-Line Tools

Let's embark on a journey into the realm of network mastery using the power of the Linux command line. Networks are the lifeblood of modern computing, and with the right tools, your command line becomes a powerful hub to diagnose issues, monitor traffic, and secure your connections.

The Foundation: Essential Network Utilities

1. **ip (iproute2):** The Swiss army knife of modern network configuration and information.
   - **Examples:**
     - `ip addr show` (lists network interfaces and their addresses)
     - `ip route show` (displays the routing table)
2. **ping:** The classic connectivity test. Sends ICMP echo packets to a host.
   - **Example:** `ping 8.8.8.8` (tests connectivity to Google's DNS server)
3. **traceroute:** Traces the network path (hops) between your system and a destination host. Invaluable for pinpointing routing problems.
   - **Example:** `traceroute www.google.com`
4. **hostname -I :** Quickly reveal your machine's IP address(es).
5. **ifconfig:** A legacy utility (partially replaced by 'ip'). Still useful in some distributions.

Deep Dives into Network Data

1. **netstat:** A versatile network status viewer. Provides information on:
   - Open ports and their state (`netstat -lt` - listening TCP ports)
   - Active connections (`netstat -at` - all TCP connections)
   - Routing table (`netstat -r`)
   - Network interface statistics (`netstat -i`)
2. **ss:** A 'successor' to netstat. Often faster and more detailed output.
   - **Example:** `ss -tulpen` (shows listening and established TCP and UDP sockets with process names and ID)

3. **tcpdump:** The low-level packet sniffer. Captures and displays network traffic in extreme detail. For advanced analysis and debugging.
4. **nmap** (covered earlier, revisited): Primarily a port scanner, but also performs host discovery, OS fingerprinting. Incredibly powerful in the right hands.

Remote Connections and File Transfers

1. **ssh:** Secure Shell. The cornerstone for encrypted remote logins and terminal sessions.
   - **Example:** `ssh user@remote_server_ip`
2. **scp:** Secure Copy. File transfers over SSH.
   - **Example:** `scp local_file.txt user@remote_server_ip:/path/on/server`
3. **rsync:** Advanced synchronization tool. Efficiently transfers only *differences* in files or directories, ideal for backups and mirroring.

Web Debugging

1. **curl:** Fetches data or makes requests to web servers (HTTP, HTTPS, FTP, and more). Downloading files, testing APIs... incredibly versatile.
2. **wget:** Non-interactive file downloader. Great for retrieving files or mirroring parts of websites.

DNS: The Address Book of the Internet

1. **dig:** Detailed DNS lookups, reveals various record types (A, AAAA, MX, etc.).
   - **Example:** `dig google.com mx` (shows mail exchanger records for google.com)
2. **host:** A simpler DNS lookup tool.
   - **Example:** `host google.com`

Additional Resources

- **ExplainShell** (https://explainshell.com/): Breaks down complex command-line usage examples.
- **Linux Networking Cookbook** ([invalid URL removed])

Troubleshooting Tips

- **Start Simple:** Use `ping` first to test basic reachability

- **Check Your Interfaces**: `ip addr show` ensures your network interfaces are up and have correct IP addresses.
- **Examine the Route**: `traceroute` to a problematic destination might reveal where packets get stuck.
- **Firewalls:** Both your local firewall (`iptables` or `ufw`) and firewalls on remote systems can block connections.

Security Considerations

- **Open Ports:** Use `netstat` or `ss` to check what services are listening on your system. Close unnecessary ones.
- **SSH Best Practices:** Disable password logins in favor of key-based authentication to greatly enhance security.
- **Firewall:** Consider a tool like `iptables` or `ufw` to control incoming and outgoing traffic.

Practical Network Analysis: A Scenario

You're experiencing slow internet speeds. Let's use command-line tools to investigate!

1. **Basics:** `ping 8.8.8.8` checks for packet loss or high latency.
2. **Gateway:** `traceroute 8.8.8.8` - are there slow hops within your local network?
3. **DNS:** `dig google.com @1.1.1.1` - test a different DNS server (like Cloudflare's) to rule out DNS resolution issues.

Conclusion

Let's conclude our epic journey into the world of the Linux command line! Think back to where you started: perhaps a little apprehensive, a bit bewildered by the blinking cursor. Now, look at yourself! You wield a powerful arsenal of commands, navigate the file system like a pro, and have the tools to bend Linux to your will.

The Power Unleashed

The command line offers unparalleled control and efficiency. Consider everything you've conquered:

- **File Manipulation:** Creating, deleting, moving, copying – entire directories restructured with a few keystrokes.
- **System Insights:** You don't just use your machine; you understand how it ticks with resource monitoring and troubleshooting abilities.
- **Customization:** Aliases and scripting let you make the terminal experience your own.
- **Problem-Solving:** Confronted with an issue, you don't search for GUI buttons; you think of what command can get the job done.
- **Unleashed Potential:** Linux is incredibly vast. The command line is the key to exploring its depths.

The Journey Continues

Linux mastery is an ongoing pursuit. Here's how to keep the momentum going:

- **Don't Fear the Unknown:** See a new command in a forum post? Experiment! Remember those valuable resources: man pages, `--help` flags, and the helpful online community.
- **Automate the Tedious:** Notice those repetitive tasks? Chances are, there's a way to script or alias them into streamlined workflows.
- **Specialized Knowledge:** Dive into the tools for your specific needs – text editing, networking, system administration – there's always a powerful command-line way.
- **Share Your Discoveries:** Help others embark on their own command-line journey. Teaching reinforces your knowledge, and new perspectives lead to new insights.

The Command Line as a Mindset

Beyond specific commands, you've cultivated powerful problem-solving habits:

- **Precision:** The command line demands attention to detail, fostering a meticulous approach.
- **Breaking Things Down:** Complex tasks become a series of interconnected commands, each part conquerable.
- **Resourcefulness:** You know how to find answers, how to experiment, and how to troubleshoot through iteration.

These transfer to far more than just your Linux system!

A Transformative Experience

Using the command line has reshaped the way you interact with your computer. There's an undeniable satisfaction in the raw power and flexibility at your fingertips, a sense of deeper understanding. This isn't just about *using* Linux, but about becoming a fluent participant in its open-source ecosystem.

Embracing the Command Line's Potential

The command line is your gateway to:

- Configuring servers in the cloud, building the backbone of the internet.
- Automating development workflows for seamless testing and deployment.
- Administering large networks, ensuring connectivity for many.
- Analyzing massive datasets with a speed and precision GUI tools often can't match.

The possibilities are as boundless as Linux itself.

Call to Action

Think of one task you currently do using mostly graphical programs. Is there a command-line way to do it, or parts of it? Start exploring, and I guarantee you'll discover unexpected power. If you get stuck, don't worry – remember, the Linux community is ready to help!

Thank you for joining me on this command-line adventure. May your terminal journey be filled with success and the sheer joy of discovery!

www.ingramcontent.com/pod-product-compliance
Lightning Source LLC
Chambersburg PA
CBHW080527060326
40690CB00022B/5052